OM GĀYATRĪ AND SANDHYĀ

by

Svāmī Mukhyānanda

Sri Ramakrishna Math
MYLAPORE MADRAS 600 004

Published by
Adhyaksha
Sri Ramakrishna Math
Mylapore, Chennai-4

Total number of copies printed before 82,800

XX-2M 5C-7-2011
ISBN 81-7120-166-0

Printed in India at
Sri Ramakrishna Math Printing Press
Mylapore, Chennai-4

Publisher's Preface

All the great religions of the world have recognised that prayer is the link between man engrossed in the concerns of life and the Supreme Being, of whom himself and the universe are the shadows, emanations or creations. The large Muslim community of the world has got the Namaz, which has to be uttered and contemplated upon five times a day. A very large cross section of them practise it at least twice a day. Similarly the Christians have got the Lord's Common Prayer.

The followers of the Vedas too have a prayer corresponding to these, and that is Gāyatrī Mantra with Sandhyā Upāsanā, to be done three times a day. It is however true that not all those who are classed as Hindus — by which expression is meant persons who profess allegiance to the Vedas — are considered eligible by the tradition in practice for the performance of the Sandhyā Upāsanā and the Gāyatrī Mantra. It is shown on pp. 48 and 49 of this book that this exclusion has no sanction of the Veda and the Smṛti of Manu. One can therefore say with much justification that the Gāyatrī and Sandhyā form the universal prayer for all Hindus.

But the unfortunate situation today is that even those who are considered eligible by tradition for this prayer, have woefully begun to neglect it. A time was when a Brāhmaṇa who failed to observe the Sandhyā was considered a Patita (fallen one) and only a Brahma-bandhu (a nominal Brāhmaṇa). But such feelings have disappeared among large sections of them. To some extent this is mainly due to the mere formality, without any understanding of the meaning, to which these practices have been reduced in the hands of the orthodoxically minded people who practise them. Among those who observe the practice, it is rare to find one who knows even the simple meaning of the Gāyatrī. Their attention is more on the external limbs (Aṅgas) of the practice, than on the core of it, namely repetition of the Gāyatrī Mantra with concentration on its meaning.

The object of this book is to bring to the earnestly-minded people the unique significance and the deep philosophy behind the Gāyatrī Mantra and the Sandhyā Upāsanā. The learned author has dealt with these in depth, giving the philosophic significance of their practices and their pragmatic value. There may be some who are not able to go all the way with him in understanding these and will be satisfied with the simple meaning of Om and the

Gāyatrī and the Sandhyā. We would like to draw the attention of such readers to pp.9-13, and 39 for the symbolism of Om, and to pp.17, 18 and 28 as also pp.54, 55, 72 & 73 for the other subjects.

For the benefit of those who want to perform Sandhyā in the orthodox style, we have given in Part III the complete details regarding the Mantras to be chanted, and the procedures to be adopted, in Devanagari script with transliteration and English translation. There will be minor variations in these practices adopted by the followers of the different Vedas. As the majority are the followers of the Yajur Veda, we have adopted their tradition in this book.

Sri Ramakrishna Math **Publisher**
Mylapore, Madras 600 004
August, 1989

Contents

KEY TO TRANSLITERATION AND PRONUNCIATION

		Sounds like
अ	a	o in son
आ	ā	a in master
इ	i	i in if
ई	ī	ee in feel
उ	u	u in full
ऊ	ū	oo in boot
ऋ	ṛ	somewhat between r an ri
ए	e	ay in May
ऐ	ai	y in my
ओ	o	o in oh
औ	au	ow in now
क	k	k in keen
ख	kh	ckh in blockhead
ग	g	g (hard) in go
घ	gh	gh in ghee
ङ	ṅ	ng in singer
च	c	ch (not k) chain
छ	ch	chh in catch him
ज	j	j in judge
झ	jh	dgeh in hedgehog
ञ	ñ	n (somewhat) as in French
ट	ṭ	t tn ten

		Sounds like
ठ	ṭh	th in ant-hill
ड	ḍ	d in den
ढ	ḍh	dh in godhood
ण	ṇ	n in under
त	t	t in French
थ	th	th in thumb
द	d	th in then
ध	dh	then in breathe
न	n	n in not
प	p	p in pen
फ	ph	ph in loop-hole
ब	b	b in bag
भ	bh	bh in abhor
म	m	m in mother
य	y	y in yard
र	r	r in run
ल	l	l in luck
व	v	v in avert
श	ś	sh in reich (German)
ष	ṣ	sh in show
स	s	s in sun
ह	h	in hot
	ṁ	m in sum
:	ḥ	h in half

FOREWORD

The First Edition of the 'Symbolism of Om and the Gayatri-Mantra', published as No.7 in the Hinduism Booklets Series on 7th September 1985 (Janmāṣṭami Day) by the Centre for Reshaping Our World-View, Calcutta, for the Centre for the Diffusion of the Light of Sanātana Dharma, became very popular both in India and abroad, and soon a reprint was called for. When the author was contemplating bringing out a revised Second Edition, it was felt that it would receive a wider circle of readers if the booklet were published by a Centre of the Ramakrishna Math.

The Ramakrishna Math, Madras, has now kindly accepted the proposal to publish the Second Edition and suggested to the author to add a few pages on the significance of the Sandhyā-Upāsana in which the Japa of the Gāyatri-Mantra forms the essential core. Accordingly, a chapter has been added on Sandhyā-Upāsana as Part II of the booklet, and the earlier portion has been slightly revised and is being published as Part I. For the convenience of those who intend to use the book for the actual performance of the Sandhya, a Part III also has been added which gives complete details regarding the mantras and the procedures to be adopted. The title of the booklet also has been amplified into 'Symbolism of Om and the Gāyatri and Sandhyā Upāsanas'. The copyright of the book too is now passed on to Sri Ramakrishna Math, Madras.

It is hoped that this edition will prove of benefit to a wider circle of people.

1st January 1989 SVĀMĪ MUKHYĀNANDĀ
KALPATARU DAY
BELUR MATH (W.B.)

Part I
Symbolism of Om (Aum) and the Gāyatrī Mantra

I The Total Existential Reality

OM or AUM is the most comprehensive, universal, non-personal, holy Sound-symbol (Logos) and Signifier (Vācaka) of the Supreme Infinite Divine Reality. This Divine Reality is of the nature of Ananta-sat-cit-ānanda (Absolute Infinite-Existence-Consciousness-Bliss). It manifests as the Totality of Existence, — from the external-most physical to the internal-most spiritual —, on four cosmic planes, Macrocosmic (Universal) as well as Microcosmic (Individual), viz. —

1. The Gross or Physical;
2. The Subtle or Psychical;
3. The Potential or Causal; and
4. The Transcendental or Meta-phenomenal, which is the source of the first three.

The first three planes are represented on the cosmic level, respectively, by:—

1. Our external physical or empirical universe of sense-experience, with its different types of life, such

as microbes, plants, fish birds, animals, human beings etc., experienced by us while living in our gross-body, — designated as Bhū or Bhūr-loka;

2. The intermediate subtle regions, with the Manes and other subtle invisible beings inhabiting them, which are apprehended by us psychically, while living, or through the subtle-body after death — , designated Bhuvaḥ, or Bhuvar-loka;

3. The several heavens, with the different types of angels and gods residing in them, including the highest heaven called the Abode of Truth (Satya-loka) where dwells the Supreme Creator-God (Brahmā the Sṛṣṭi-kartā) of these three planes, to be envisioned by us spiritually in different levels of Samadhi or Trance, while living, or through the spiritual-body after death — designated as Svaḥ or Svar-Loka.

These three planes (Tri-bhuvana) together constitute the entire phenomenal Cosmic Universe, called the Brahmāṇḍa. The Supreme Being, the Cosmic Soul of the entire Brahmāṇḍa and all its beings, is designated Parama-Īśvara (the Supreme Lord and Ruler). Parama-Īśvara (Parameśvara) rules this Brahamāṇḍa, divided into fourteen Cosmic Worlds (Caturdaśa-bhuvana or Lokas),[1] from within

(Antar-yāmin) permeating it as its Over-soul (Paramātmā).

Beyond the phenomenal Brahmāṇḍa is the Noumenal, Non-Personal, transcendental absolute spiritual reality designated Brahman (the Infinite), which is Supra-corporeal, Meta-physical, and beyond all the worlds and heavens (Lokātīta). That is the fourth plane (Turīya), the Absolute beyond all time, space and causation. It is pure infinite spiritual existence, with consciousness and bliss as its very nature, and not any Region or Person. All the other three planes are relative. They are within time, space, and causation, and rest on the Fourth, their Source, like a cinema-show on the screen without affecting It. It is the Absolute Brahman that appears as Parameśvara when associated with the Brahmāṇḍa or the entire phenomenal universe of the three planes.

II The Macrocosm and the Microcosm

The Macrocosm, which is represented by all the above four cosmic planes, and the Microcosm or the individual unit which is a part of it, are built on the same plan, just like the fully manifested tree with its trunk and branches, leaves, flowers, and fruits which also bear seeds, each of which contains within itself the potentiality of manifesting a similar whole tree, including similar seeds. Though the seeds are for the time being a very minor part of the tree, without any similarity to it, all the elements and ingredients of the whole tree are lying latent within every seed, though invisible. Similarly, each individual being or person, though apparently an insignificant part of the Brahmāṇḍa, contains the potentiality of the entire four planes of existence of Ananta-sat-cit-ānanda, which he or she can manifest in due course through spiritual efforts (Sādhana) and find affinity and unity (Yoga) on each Cosmic Plane through identification with it. Hence, as a corollary and correlate to Brahmāṇḍa, the individual is called the Piṇḍāṇḍa, Aṇḍa meaning egg, which has the potentiality of reproducing its original source.

It will be interesting to note that from the Vedic literature onwards in the Upaniṣads, the Smṛtis and the later Sanskrit literature — the supreme divine reality Brahman is referred to as the eternal empyrean source in which the Tree of the Universe, called Aśvattha (literally, that which will not last till tomorrow', that is, ever-changing and ephemeral), is rooted.[2] The universe continuously manifests from the Reality, like the waves in the ocean, while the Reality remains unchanging. Sometimes, the Divine Reality itself, along with the universe, is referred to as the Eternal Tree, since the universe and its beings are rooted in It. The Chāndogya Upaniṣad (VI.8.4) says: "All these entities and creatures, my dear, have Being (Sat) as their root, have Being as their abode and have Being as their support. (Sat-mūlaḥ saumya imāḥ sarvāḥ prajāḥ, Satāyatanāḥ, Sat-pratiṣṭhāḥ). The Kaṭha Upaniṣad (VI.1) says: "This is the Eternal Aśvattha Tree whose roots are above and whose branches spread below. That is verily the Pure, that is Brahman, and that is also called the Immortal. In that rest all the worlds, and none can transcend it. Verily this is That." In the *Śvestāśvatara Upaniṣad* III.9, we find: "Rooted in His own glory He stands like a Tree — One without a second and immovable. By that Being the whole universe is filled." The Gītā (XV 1-3) echoes the Kaṭha: "They speak of an immutable eternal Aśvattha rooted above and branching below whose leaves are the Vedas; he who knows it is a knower of the Veda..."

It was stated above that whatever is in the Macrocosm in a fully developed form is also in the Microcosm potentially in the seed-form, though unseen. Conversely, we may also surmise that whatever latent physical, mental, aesthetic, and other faculties are manifested and developed in the Microcosm in course of time or of evolution, are already present in the Macrocosm in a fully developed state, though ordinarily invisible to us.[3] That is, we cannot comprehend them without proper mental equipment, training and attuning of ourselves to it. But the Yogis with disciplined and trained minds, visualise them (Yogi-pratyakṣa), just as, what ordinarily we cannot see with bare eyes, the astronomers see about the far away galaxies, nebulae, etc. with the help of powerful telescopes. The Ṛg-Veda declares: "The illumined sages (Sūrayaḥ) constantly see that infinite all-pervading Supreme Reality (Viṣṇu) without any obstruction, as though their vast intuitive eye (vision) was spread out in the spiritual sky."[4] And the Kaṭha Upaniṣad points out, "This Atman, hidden in the hearts of all beings, is not ordinarily revealed to all; but it is verily revealed to the subtle and pointed (concentrated) intellect of the sages who are trained in perceiving subtle objects."[4(a)]

On the Microcosmic level, in the individual person, the corresponding states of the Four Cosmic planes are:

1. The gross or physical-body (Sthūla-Śarīra) of the waking-state (Jāgrat) operative while living, which is an integral part of our entire physical universe of sense-perception (Bhūḥ).

2. The subtle or psychic-body (Sūkṣma-Sarīra), experienced psychically and to some extent in the dream-state (Svapna), which survives the death of the

gross-body and is an integral part of the cosmic psychic-plane (Bhuvaḥ).

3.The potential or causal-body (Kāraṇa-śarīra): experienced as the formless and objectless pure peaceful happiness in the dreamless deep-sleep-state (Suṣupti), when both the gross-body and the subtle-body, with all their Samskāras (stored up impressions) are held in abeyance, and which lasts till the real Self-Knowledge dawns. It is equivalent to the state of involution (Prati-sarga) of Brahmāṇḍa, when it returns by the reverse process into its causal or seed-state (Pralaya) after billions of billion years. From that seed-state again the evolution (Sarga) of the next universe commences after a long period of dynamic rest, just as we commence our next day after sleep.

In the different categories of spiritual states experienced in different types of trances and Samādhis, when one envisions angels, gods, and the supreme Personal Creator-God and has communication with them, the causal-body, having been purified and rendered subtler, placid and transparent (Sāttvika) by spiritual Sādhana, manifests as a spiritual body (Sattvika-śarīra) or Divinised-Body (Bhāgavatī-tanu), which is an integral part of the cosmic heavens (Svaḥ).

These three are the phenomenal states of the individual person, corresponding to the cosmic phenomenal universe. The spiritual entity within the person which endows the body with personality and consciousness, enabling it to get all the experiences of life in all the states, is called the Jīva or Jivātman. The Jīvatman is the Lord and ruler of the body and controls and guides it from within, even as Paramātman controls the universe, which is like a body to Him, from within it.[5]

4. The Fourth Plane (Turīya) on the individual level is the Absolute Atman, corresponding to Absolute Brahman, realised only in Nirvikalpa-Samādhi (Transcendental Trance) when the mind merges in the Spirit, its source, beyond all manifested and potential corporeality. It is the Absolute Ātman which appears as the Jīva when associated with individual beings. The individual personality and life rest on the Ātman like the cinema-show on the screen without affecting it. On this plane the Ātman is identical with Brahman, since it is a plane beyond all phenomena, beyond Brahmāṇḍa, where there is no time, space or causation to bring about division or limitation in any manner in the pure infinite spiritual existence.

Thus every individual contains all aspects of the whole of existence, from the grossest physical to the subtlest spiritual, in a potential form. What is more, everyone can realize it with appropriate spiritual efforts (Sādhana). And the Upāsana or meditation on Om is one of the chief and effective means of realizing it.

III Om as Auditory Symbol

Om is primarily an auditory or sound-symbol. It represents in a nutshell all the above four planes of the supreme infinite divine Reality, both Macrocosmically and Microcosmically, for purposes of meditation to help visualize and realize their unity in life. The symbolism is explained here briefly.

All our experiences of entities and ideas in all the states of consciousness are represented by words, and they are so fused together that we cannot recall or think of any entity or idea without words. Words are made up of unit-sounds, such as are denoted by A to Z of the alphabet in English. With these sounds we form all our words and concepts. So A to Z can be in a way a symbol of the knowledge of the whole of Reality. For example, we say, 'He knows from A to Z of a particular thing.' But the Roman alphabet is incomplete and defective. For, in this alphabet system the same letter represents different sounds in different contexts, and more than one letter is used to represent certain sounds. Its arrangement too is casual and unscientific, and its pronunciation and use in words is erratic.

In Sanskrit, each unit-sound is represented by a single definite letter, and the pronunciation and spelling of the letters are always the same. For example, in Sanskrit the consonant 'k' (क्) with the vowel 'a' (अ) added (as in Karma) is pronounced as 'Ka' and spelt also as 'Ka' (क) only. But in English we pronounce it as 'Ka', and spell it as Kay-Ye. The Sanskrit alphabet is arranged in accordance with the order of origination of sounds in the vocal system, commencing from the larynx with the opening of the mouth, passing through the throat, and ending with the closing of the lips, by the contact of different parts of the mouth with the tongue. Between opening and closing of the mouth we produce all the words which represent all our experiences and concepts. When we open the mouth, we utter 'a' (pronounced like 'o' in come) and when we close the lips, we utter 'm' (again like 'm' in come).[6] Thus between 'a' and 'm' come all the other sounds and words that are uttered. Inserting in the middle the vowel 'u' (like 'u' in full), which rolls through the throat over the whole tongue, we cover the entire beginning, middle, and end of all words symbolically.

In Sanskrit when 'a' and 'u' are combined, it gives us the sound 'o' as in go, and adding 'm' to it we get the Om. Now the 'a' 'u' 'm', known as Mātras (phonetic constituents) of Om, are symbolic not only of the beginning, middle, and end of all the words, and of the entities and concepts represented by them, but of all the worlds (Lokas) as well for purposes of meditation. They represent the three planes of Bhūḥ, Bhuvaḥ, and Svaḥ and the corresponding Microcosmic States. When Om is uttered mystically, the inarticulate humming sound that lingers (as after a gong is sounded), designated as the Ardha-mātra or a-Mātra (half or non-Matra), known also as the Anāhata-dhvani (Unstruck-sound or the Eternal Nāda) represents the Absolute beyond the worlds (Lokottara) or the Fourth Plane (Turīya). Thus Aum is symbolic of the entire existence, phenomenal as well as the noumenal, Macrocosmic as well as Microcosmic, Personal Iśvara as well as Impersonal or Trans-personal Brahman-Ātman. Hence Om, called also as Praṇava, is considered as the fitting designation or signifier of the infinite supreme Divine Reality (*Tasya vācakaḥ praṇavaḥ*), and is held to be the holiest universal Name. Hence Om is also characterised as Śabda-Brahman (Sound-Brahman or Brahman in the form of Sound or the Word). Om being the universal Cosmic Sound (the Logos), the totality of all sounds, it is called Praṇava (the primordial Reverberating Sound which fills the Universe), from which, modified as the Akāśa (Space/Matter), the subtle and gross universe with all its entities and beings evolves in stages. Often 'Om Tat Sat' (Om that Existence or Reality) is uttered to indicate the transcendental aspect of Divine Existence. (Cf. *Om-Tat-Sattiti nirdeśo Brahmaṇaḥ trividhaḥ smṛtaḥ* — Gītā, XVII.23).

IV The Om (Aum) as an Audio-Visual Symbol

The figure of Om given in the cover page of this book is a graphic symbol of it for ritualistic purposes and to indicate its correct utterance in Mantra combinations as Bījākṣara. In literary usage Om is written in one of these two forms: ओं or ओम्. The symbolic form of it is: (ॐ) In this the front two curves, one above and the other below in the figure, represent 'a' and 'u', the Bhūr-Loka (the gross plane) and the Bhuvar-loka (the subtle plane), respectively. The curve projecting from their middle resembling the trunk of an elephant, represents 'm', the Suvar-Loka (the causal plane), whence the Praṇava (the Logos) issues forth reverberating, as if from the trunk of an elephant. The small curve with the dot above the curved trunk, known as Candra-bindu, signifying in Sanskrit the semi-nasal sound, represents the inarticulate lingering sound, when Om is pronounced mystically as prescribed. It is just like the lingering sound after a gong is sounded. It stands for the Absolute. Words, and the 'Worlds' which are their concretized aspects, issue forth unceasingly from the cosmic Oṁ-kāra (Sound Om) like waves in the sea.

This graphic symbol of Om was, in course of time, further concretized and personified for purposes of Upāsana into the figure of the Deity Gajānana (The Elephant-Faced Deity; Gaja=elephant, Ānana=face) or Gaṇeśa (the Lord of all Bhūta-gaṇas or Cosmic Elements: Īśa = Lord or Ruler of the Bhūtas or elements, Gaṇa = group). All the holy and auspicious attributes and functions that were associated with Om from the Vedic times were transferred to Him. His figure is a philosophic symbol to which suitable mythology was later added to explain His figure popularly. We shall not go into the details of this highly interesting and profound cosmic symbolism here, but only hint at the fact that His pot-belly signifies that the whole Brahmāṇda is within Him, and He stands transcending it. The similarity of the elephant-face and the figure of the Om is quite evident. He easily rides or controls the troublesome Māya, represented by the small but mischievous mouse, His mount. All this is in keeping with the Hindu tradition of symbolically concretizing and personifying abstract entities as already mentioned. Gaṇeśa is often referred to as Om-kāra-svarūpa (of the form of Om). We may also note here that in the Hindu Pantheon all the Deities have animals as their vehicles, signifying divine powers controlling animal tendencies.

V Aum and Spiritual Practice

To help in spiritual practice (Upāsana), A U M, the phonetic constituents of Om, are identified with different types of Cosmic Triads, from the theistic to the philosophic and the mystic levels, for meditation purposes according to the need and development of the aspirant.[7] Further, Om being the Praṇava (Cosmic-Sound), the Logos in the Divine Mind, it is from It that all the concepts of the universe and its entities arise and take shape as existent entities. By the mystic repetition of the Om, one attunes oneself to the Cosmic Mind and is lifted up spiritually. By connecting oneself mentally to the cosmic reservoir through Upāsana, one's mind becomes a conduit for the flow of inspiration from the Cosmic Mind. Hence it is considered the holiest Mantra (mystic formula) for Japa (sacred repetition) and is, therefore, added at the beginning of all other Mantras used for Japa.

Let us take two examples to see how the symbolism works psychologically:

1. The script we use for any language is nothing but an artificially contrived arbitrary device — a set of symbols to record sounds. Still it helps us to store knowledge, which in itself is non-material, in books. One who knows a language well and has learnt the particular script, to him is opened all the knowledge stored in all the books in that language, though he may still need the help of the learned. Similarly, if one knows the symbolism of Om, and all the ideas it represents, to him is open all the Divine Knowledge, which he may realize with the help of a Guru.

2. Suppose we have forgotten the name of a person about whom we want to communicate to a friend. We begin to give various details and descriptions; still it may not give an adequate or correct idea of the person. The friend's mind being in doubt, he does not feel any attraction to him. On the other hand, suppose we utter the name of a person, say Śrī Rāmakṛṣṇa or Jesus Christ, immediately in the mind of a person who has intimate knowledge about him, the cumulative effect of all his knowledge brings about a sense of love and reverence. Then, if the context needs, he may begin to recount all the details of that great life. Similarly, if a person has learnt all about the infinite supreme Divinity from the scriptures and the Guru and that Om is Its designation , as soon as he utters Om all

the greatness of that Divinity and Its wonderful manifestations come to his mind with a cumulative force and uplifts him. Then he may begin to contemplate on the details intensely and intimately, associating himself with It at all levels. This intimate intense contemplation is called Upāsana, which literally means 'sitting or placing oneself mentally near' to the object of meditation. The psychological law is '*Yat dhyāyati tat bhavati*' (whatever one contemplates or meditates upon intensely, that he becomes). The more one recalls the name of a person whom he loves, the nearer one feels to him and clearer he visualizes him. Similarly, the more one repeats Om with the requisite attitude, the more one recalls the infinite supreme Divinity, and feels close to it. Ultimately he realizes his essential identity with It, since he is, as we saw, potentially the microcosmic counterpart of It.[8]

In ritualistic worship the identification of the macrocosm and microcosm is mentally visualized by a process called Nyāsa which consists of touching different parts of the body while uttering the words of the cosmic counterparts. In Mānasa-pūjā or Mental-worship too symbolic identification is mentally contemplated.

VI The Gāyatrī-Mantra

The Gāyatrī-Mantra is the greatest prayer-Mantra which incorporates all the ideas of the Om-symbolism. It is a prayer to the supreme infinite Divine Reality for the enlightenment of the Intelligence(Dhi) of all human beings to enable them to realize the Supreme Truth. It is also known as the Sāvitrī-Mantra, since it is addressed to the Divine Person in the Sun, (Savitā) who is considered as the visible symbolic representation of the Supreme Divinity. For, He destroys darkness and promotes life, and He is also identified with the Inner Self of man. (Cf. Īśa Upaniṣad. 15-16).

Sāvitrī signifies that which is related to Savitṛ (Savitā) which means the source or originator of the universe, as well as the sun. The Sāvitrī-Mantra is composed in the Gāyatrī metre, and it being the best and most significant of Mantras in that metre it has become famous as the Gāyatrī. This Mantra occurs in the Vedas (Ṛg-Veda. III.62.10) and is considered to be their very essence, or even their Mother (Gāyatrī Veda-mātā). Later on Gāyatrī was associated with Om, which is also considered as the source of the Vedas. Through this interconnection Gāyatrī was treated as the elaboration of Om. Om was prefixed to it along with the three Vyāhṛtis,[9] which are utterances of the Divine Creator representing the three Cosmic Planes, Bhūr-Bhuvaḥ-Svaḥ (Cf. Bṛhadāraṇyaka Upaniṣad. V.14. 1-8; and Chāndogya Upaniṣad. II.-23.2-3, III.12 [10]) The Gāyatrī-Mantra in full, repeated mystically, runs as follows

OM BHŪR-BHUVAḤ-SUVAḤ
TAT-SAVITUR-VAREṆYAM
BHARGO DEVASYA DHĪMAHI
DHIYO YO NAḤ PRACODAYĀT

(Om, we meditate (*Dhīmahi*) on the Spiritual Effulgence (*Bhargas*) of that Adorable Supreme Divine Reality (*Vareṇyam Devasya*), the Source or Projector (*Savitṛ*) of the three phenomenal world-planes — the gross or physical (*Bhūḥ*),the subtle or psychical (*Bhuvaḥ*), and the potential or causal (*Suvaḥ*), both macrocosmically (externally) and microcosmically (internally). May that Supreme Divine Being (*Tat*) stimulate (*Pracodayāt*) our (*Naḥ*) intelligence (*Dhiyah*), so that we may realize the Supreme Truth.")

The Gāyatrī-Mantra is the most universal, non-personal, holy prayer which can be used by any person belonging to any country, irrespective of race, religion, or sex. If one is a human being with intelligence — that is qualification enough for repeating this Prayer-mantra.

In course of time, just as the Oṁ-kāra was personified into Gaṇeśa, the Gāyatrī-Mantra also was personified into the Goddess Gāyatrī (Gāyatrī-Devī), as the presiding Deity of the Mantra, for purposes of Personal Upāsana (Saguṇa-upasana). The following verse is repeated in adoration as a Dhyāna-śloka (invocatory meditational verse):

Muktā-vidruma-hema-nīla-dhavala-cchāyair-
mukhair-tryakṣaṇaiḥ
Yuktām indu-nibaddha-ratna-mukutām
tattvārtha varṇātmikām
Gayatrīm varadābhayāṅkuśa-kaśām
śubhram-kapālam-gadām
Śankham-cakram athāravinda-yugalam
hastair-vahantīm bhaje.

(I adore the Goddess Gāyatrī, the embodiment of the Varṇas (letters of the alphabet) signifying the Supreme Truth, with Her five benign faces reflecting the hues of pearls, corals, gold, sapphire, and snow—each face studded with three eyes (denoting omniscience) — , whose head is adorned with a jewelled crown crested with the crescent-moon, whose two hands (out of ten, representing omnipotence) are in the pose of bestowing boons and fearlessness, and who in her other hands holds the goad, the whip, the white-skull, the mace, the conch, and the discus (as symbols of terror to the evil forces), and a pair of lotuses (as symbols of purity, love, devotion, and detachment). Cf. also Devi-Mahatmya or Chandi I.73-74: IV.10.

VII Importance of Om and the Gāyatrī

Om and the Gāyatri-Mantra have acquired such great importance that they are often referred to as *the Praṇava* and *the Gāyatrī* just as the Bhagavad-Gītā is referred to as *the Gītā.* In the Vedas, Upaniṣads, the Gītā, and the later literature, there are numerous references to the holiness, importance, and significance of the Praṇava and the Gāyatrī. The whole of the Māṇḍūkya Upaniṣad is devoted to the delineation of the spirituo-philosophical significance of Om. Though the Upaniṣad contains only twelve verses, it is considered so important that numerous commentaries are written on it. Śrī Gauḍapāda-ācārya, the grand Guru of Śrī Śaṅkarācārya, has written an extremely subtle and revolutionary philosophical work called the Māṇḍūkya-kārikā to elucidate the high philosophy of this Upaniṣad which establishes the supremacy and ultimacy of the Non-dual Reality (Advaita). Śrī Śaṅkarācārya has commented on both the Upaniṣad and the Kārikā.

We shall give here a few of the important original quotations in translation from the Upaniṣads and the Gītā referring to the Praṇava and the Gāyatri.

1. *Kaṭha Upaniṣad* (I.2. 15-17):

"The Goal which all *Vedas* proclaim, which all austerities and meditations (*Tapāmsi*) seek, and desiring which the sages lead the life of Brahmacarya (continent spiritual life) — I tell it to thee in brief — It is Om." (Cf. *Gita*, VIII. 11)

"This immortal Word (Logos) is verily Brahmā (the Personal Creator-God). This immortal Word is verily also the Highest Brahman (the Impersonal Divine Reality). Having understood this Immortal Word, whatever one desires, one gets that."

"This Support (Om as a means of realization of Brahman) is the best; This Support is the Supreme. Knowing this Support (realizing the Truth signified by Om), one is exalted in the World of Brahmā."

2. *Praśna Upaniṣad* (The whole of Section V), some verses only are quoted here (V. 2-5, 7):

"What is Om, O Satyakāma, is verily the Higher or Transcendental (Impersonal) Brahman and the Relative or Phenomenal (Personal) Creator-God Brahmā. Therefore the Knower attains either of the two by this means."

"If one meditates upon only one of the three Mātra-s (Moras) of Om, he comes back to this world very soon (after his death), being enlightened by that. The *Ṛk* Hymns lead him to the world of man, where he attains greatness (in life), being endowed with austerity (Tapasya), continence (Brahmacarya), and faith (Śraddhā)."

"If again, one meditates upon two Mātra-s, one is united with the mind (after death). He is led to the World of the Moon (the presiding Deity of the mind) in the Intermediate Region, by the Yajus Formulas. And there in that world of Moon, having enjoyed its grandeur, he comes back again."

"Again, he who meditates upon the Supreme Puruṣa (Parameśvara) with the Immortal Word Om, constituted of all the three Mātras, becomes united with the effulgent Sun. He is freed from all sins, even as a snake is freed from its slough. He is led to the world of Brahmā by the *Sāma* chants. Then he beholds the Supreme Puruṣa residing in the Heart, higher than this highest totality of Jīvas (Brahmā or Hiraṇyagarbha)."

"...Verily, with this Om-kāra (the *a-Matra*) as the Support, the Knower attains what is peaceful, undecaying, immortal, fearless, and supreme (Ātman/Brahman)."

3. *Muṇḍaka Upaniṣad* (II. 2, 3, 4, 6):

"Taking as bow the mighty Upaniṣadic weapon, fix on it the arrow sharpened by constant meditation. And having drawn it to the full with the mind absorbed in Its thought, penetrate that Target, my dear, the Immutable Reality."

"Praṇava (the mystic Word Om) is the bow; the Soul within, the arrow; and Brahman, the target. One should hit that mark with an undistracted mind, and like the arrow, become one with It."

"Where all the arteries meet like the spokes of a chariot-wheel in the hub — there within the (psychic) heart He moves, becoming manifold. Meditate on that Self as Om. Godspeed to you in crossing to the farther shore beyond all darkness."

4. *Māṇḍukya Upaniṣad*— The entire Upaniṣad is an exposition of Om. Here it is briefly quoted:

"All this Cosmic Universe is the Eternal Word Om. Its further explanation is this: the past, the present, the future, everything is just Om. And whatever transcends the three divisions of time — that too is just Om."(1)

"For, verily, everything is Brahman. And this Self (Ātman) within is Brahman. The Ātman has four quarters (aspects) — Waking, Dream, and Deep-sleep States of Consciouness, and Turīya or Samādhi, the Super-Conscious State." (2) ... "This Ātman is to be identified with Om, when Om is considered as a single complete Word. When Om is considered as composed of parts, the aspects of the Ātman are to be identified with the parts, and the parts with the aspects. The parts of Om are A, U, M, (to be identified with Waking, Dream, and Deep-sleep states of the Ātman). (8)..."The Immortal Word Om in its partless (i.e. inarticulate) aspect is the Fourth (Turīya) — the Transcendental, devoid of phenomenality, the Supreme Bliss, and Non-dual. Thus the Word Om is verily the Self (Ātman). He who knows this, with his self, (Jīva), enters the Self (Ātman).[12]

5. *Taittirīya Upaniṣad* (Whole of Anuvāka VIII in Chapter I, briefly quoted here):

"One should contemplate: Om is Brahman; all this universe (perceived by the senses and intuited by the mind) is Om... A Brāhmaṇa proceeding to recite the Veda, intending, 'Let me obtain the *Veda*,' says Om. Assuredly he attains Brahman."

6. *Chāndogya Upaniṣad* (A few passages are quoted here. See also I. 1. 8-9; IV. 17. 1-3):

"Now, that which is Udgīta is verily Praṇava and that which is Praṇava is Udgīta. The yonder Sun is Udgīta and also Praṇava; for He moves along pronouncing'Om'." (I.5.1)

"Prajāpati (the Vedic Lord of Creation) brooded (made Tapas or meditated) on the worlds. From them, thus brooded on, issued forth the threefold Veda and, as their essence, the Mystic Word Oṁ. Just as all the parts of the leaf are permeated by the ribs of the leaf, so are all words permeated by the Oṁ-kāra. Verily, the Oṁ-kāra is all this — yea, the Oṁ-kāra is verily all this." (II. 23. 2-3)

"Gāyatrī indeed is all this, whatever being exists. Speech indeed is Gāyatrī ; for speech indeed sings and removes fear of all that exists ... Such is the greatness of this (Gāyatrī). The Supreme Cosmic Person (Puruṣa) is even greater than this. All this Cosmic Universe is a quarter of Him, the other three quarters of Him constitute the Immortal Transcendent." (III.12.1 to 6 in brief).

7. *Bṛhadāraṇyaka Upaniṣad*:

See Sections V.14. 1-8, and VI. 36 for ritualistic and meditational application of Gāyatrī.

8. *Svetāśvatara Upaniṣad*: (I.1.4)

"Making one's own body the lower piece of wood (Araṇi) and the Praṇava the upper piece of wood (for purposes of rituals fire is kindled by rubbing two pieces of holy wood or short sticks called Araṇis), and practising churning in the form of meditation, one should realize the inherent Divine as one would find out something hidden (like fire in the Araṇis)."

9. *Maitrī Upaniṣad* (Also called Maitreyī or Maitrāyaṇī Upaniṣad): (A few passages are quoted here. See also Sections VI. 1,4,6,8, 22-26, 34, 37; and VII.5.II):

"Those two, the Spirit within and the Sun, go forth toward each other. One should reverence them with the Word Om, with the Mystic Utterances (Vyāhṛtis) — Bhūḥ, Bhuvaḥ, Svaḥ — and with the Sāvitrī (Gāyatrī) prayer."

"There are, assuredly, two forms of Brahman: the formed and the formless. Now, that which is the formed is unreal; that which is the formless is real, is Brahman, is light. That Light is the same as the Sun. Verily, That came to have Om as its Soul (Ātman). He divided Himself threefold. Om consists of three Mātras (A-U-M). By means of these the whole world is woven as with warp and woof across Him. For thus has it been said: 'One should absorb oneself meditating that the Sun is Om." (VI.2-3)

Various Triads of the forms of the Ātman, worshipped by the use of the threefold Om

"Now, it has elsewhere been said: A. U. M is the threefold form of this Atman:

A, U, M (Om)	- This is the Sound-form
Feminine, Masculine, Neuter	- This is the Sex-form
Fire, Wind, Sun	- This is Light-form
Brahmā, Rudra, and Viṣṇu;	- This is the Lordship-form
Gārhatya, Dakṣiṇāgni, and Ahavanīya Sacrifical Fires	- This is the Mouth-form - (Mouth of Gods)
Ṛg-Veda, Yajur-Veda, Sāma-Veda	- This is Understanding-form
Bhūr, Bhuvaḥ, Suvaḥ	- This is the World-form
Past, Present, Future	- This is the Time-form
Breath, Fire, and Sun	- This is heat-form
Food, Water, and Moon	- This is the Swelling-form
Intellect, Mind and Egoism	- This is the Intelligence-form
Prāṇa, Apāna and Vyāna Breaths	- This is the Breath-form

Hence these are praised, honoured, and included by saying Om. For thus has it been said: 'This

Immortal Word Om, verily, O Satyakāma, is both the Transcendental and Phenomenal Brahman." (VI.5)

Worship of the Ātman in the form of the Sun by the use of the Sāvitrī-prayer

Tat Savitur Vareṇyam (That Adorable Splendour of That Savitṛ the Originator of the Universe):

'Yonder Sun, verily is Savitṛ (a visible symbol). He, verily, is to be sought thus by one seeking Ātman' — say the expounders of Brahman.

Bhargo Devasya Dhīmahi (May we meditate upon That splendour of the Divinity):

Savitā, verily, is the Divinity. Hence upon that which is called His splendour do I meditate" — say the expounders of Brahman.

Dhiyo yo naḥ pracodayāt (And may He inspire our thoughts).

'Thoughts, verily, are meditations. And may He inspire these for us' - say the expounders of Brahman. - (VI. 7- in part).

See also Nṛsimha-Pūrva-Tāpini and Uttara-Tāpini Upaniṣads, and the Sāvitrī Upaniṣad.

10. *The Bhagavad-Gītā*:

"Controlling all the senses, confining the mind in the Heart, drawing up the Prāṇa-Vāyu (through the Suṣumnā) towards the head Sahasrāra), and thus occupied in the practice of Yoga, he who departs from the body uttering the one-syllabled Om denoting Brahman, and meditating on Me, attains the Supreme Goal." (VIII. 12-13).

The Lord says-

'Praṇavaḥ sarva Vedeṣu' - I am the Om in all the Vedas (VII.8);

'Pavitram Om-kāraḥ'— I am the Holy Word Om (IX.17)

'Girāmasmi ekam akṣaram' — of words, I am the single-syllabled word (Om) (X.25)

'Of Sāmans also I am the Bṛihat- sāman, of metres Gāyatrī am I' (X.35).

'Om, Tat, Sat', this has been declared to be the triple designation of Brahman. By that were made of old the Brāmanās, the Vedas, and the Yajnas. Therefore, uttering Om the acts of sacrifice, gift, and austerity, as enjoined in the ordinances, are always begun by the followers of the Vedas (XVII.23-24).

Mahanārāyaṇa Upaniṣad on Om and Gāyatrī:

"The One-syllabled Om is Brahman. (For this Mantra, Agni is its Deity. Its Ṛsi is also Brahman. Its metre is Gāyatrī. Its application is for the union with Paramātman (Section XXXIII).

"May the boon-conferring Divine Gāyatrī come to us (to instruct us about) the Imperishable Brahman who is revealed by the Vedanta. May Gāyatrī, the Mother of Metres, favour us with the knowledge of the Supreme Brahman." (Sec.XXXIV).

"O Gāyatrī, Thou art the vigour, Thou are the stamina, Thou art the strength, and Thou art the brilliance in all. Thou art the origin and sustenance of Gods. Thou art the Universe and its duration. Thou art all that exist and their span of life. Thou surpassest everything. Thou art the Truth denoted by the Praṇava. I invoke Thee as Gāyatrī (Giver of Illumination); I invoke Thee as Sāvitrī (Giver of Life); I invoke Thee as Sarasvati (Giver of Knowledge and Wisdom):... "(Sec.XXXV.1).

"Om Bhūh, Om Bhuvaḥ, Om Suvaḥ, Om Mahaḥ (the Regions of Spiritual Light), Om Janaḥ (the place of Origin of Universe), Om Tapaḥ (the Region of Higher Knowledge and Meditation), Om Satyam (the Abode of Truth): Om, May we meditate on the Adorable Splendour of that Supreme Divine source of All, to quicken our Understanding. Om, it is the Causal Waters, Light, Bliss, Ambrosia, Brahman, and also the Three Worlds. All these are verily Om." (Sec.XXXV.2).

NOTES

1. The Third Plane (Suvaḥ or Suvar-Loka) was later classified into Suvaḥ, Mahaḥ, Janaḥ, Tapaḥ, and Satyam, according to their subtlety. Together with the first two planes they make up the seven higher worlds. Below the first gross or physical world (Bhūr-Loka), there are also seven invisible nether worlds (Pātāla-Lokas) of demoniac nature, designated in the order of their increasing darkness: Atala, Vitala, Sutala, Rasātala, Talātala, Mahātala, and Pātāla. Both the higher and the lower worlds together make up the fourteen worlds (Caturdaśa-Bhuvana). Often the nether worlds are treated as the subtle lower (Infra) extensions of the Bhūr-Loka, just as Śuvar-Loka is classified into higher (Supra) five Lokas. Microcosmically, these seven nether worlds are considered as the sub-conscious psychic planes (as

the suffix 'tala' i.e. bottom or plane, indicates) of the seven higher planes and are not often mentioned separately. They are opposed to the inner divine forces and are to be vanquished with effort and not to be attained through Sādhana. That is why we find in Hindu mythology, gods and goddesses often fighting the demons and vanquishing them (See also Note No.5)

2. 'Aśvattha' has different meanings. In ordinary usage it is a tree belonging to the fig variety (Ficus Religiosa). In common language it is the pipal tree grown in front of temples and considered holy. It grows up to a very huge size, but its berries are very small. Its leaves have long stalks and hence the leaves are constantly in movement with the slightest breeze, even when other trees are still. Probably this has earned it the name Aśvattha. Consequently, it has served as a symbol of religio-philosophical significance. Ācārya Śaṅkara comments in the Kaṭha Up. (II.3.1) that the world is in constant movement like the Aśvattha (*Aśvatthavat nitya-pracalita-svabhāvaḥ*).

It is also a very hardy tree and, like the ego, it is very difficult to eradicate (Cf. Śrī Rāmākṛṣṇa's sayings). It grows anywhere, even on walls and windows; and if a little of the root is left, it sprouts up again. Because of its religio-philosophical association from ancient times and its great usefulness, it is considered a holy tree. Since the Buddha attained Enlightenment under this tree, it has become known as the Bodhi-tree (Boḍhi-Vṛkṣa) also. It is often seen in the villages with a big platform around it, sometimes with some holy images at its base. Being a huge spreading tree, it serves as a resting place for the travellers, and the village meetings, school etc. are also held under the shade of the tree on the platform.

3. This is the idea underlying the concept of Adhiṣṭhāna-Devatas (Presiding Deities), the Luminous (Deva from Div=to shine), Cosmic counterparts of the various faculties, arts and sciences etc. in the Hindu tradition and thought. These Luminous Devatas, formless but conscious, like the mind. were later on endowed with concrete personified philosophico-mythological forms - for purposes of adoration and worship (Upāsana), to invoke those qualities in oneself in a greater measure. This tendency to concretize and personify the abstract and the formless is an uniquely special feature of Hindu tradition from the Vedic times to the present day in all fields of life — especially in the religious and aesthetic fields. (Cf. the Seasons, and the Ragaṣ and

Raginis of music, personified in plastic art and painting). The Devatas were step by step raised higher and higher and ultimately identified with the ultimate supreme Divine Reality, of which they are but aspectual expressions.

4. *Tad-viṣṇoḥ paramam padam sadā paśyanti sūrayaḥ; divī-iva cakṣur-ātatam* — *Ṛg-Veda,* I.22.20

4a. *Eṣa sarveṣu bhūteṣu guḍho ātmā na prakāśate, Dṛśyate tu agryayā buddhyā sukṣmayā sūkṣma-darśibhiḥ* — *Kaṭha Upaniṣad,* III.12

5. Just as the Brahmāṇḍa has fourteen cosmic worlds or Lokas, the body also has correspondingly fourteen microcosmic subtle psychic centres called Cakras or Padmas (Lotuses), the higher seven being arranged along the spine at different levels, roughly indicated by the various plexuses. However, these Cakras and the Sahasrāra Padma are located in the subtle-body. Though six of them (Ṣaḍ-cakras) are well known, there are intervening other Cakras as well. The lower seven Cakras are below the Mūladhāra Lotus, as it were in its stalk, in the coccyx or, according to some in the region where the legs commence(Padādi). (See,'The Serpent Power' by Sir John Woodroffe). V.S. Apte, in his 'The Practical Sanskrit-English Dictionary', quotes under the word Nāḍi, from Malati-Mādhava (5.1.2),

'*Ṣaḍ-adhika-daśa-nāḍī-cakra-madhya sthit-ātma* — The Atman abiding in the midst of the sixteen Nāḍi-cakras. When one's Psychic Energy (Prāṇavāyu) is raised along the central Psychic-channel (Suṣumnā-Nāḍi) in the spine (in the subtle-body), from bottom upwards, through appropriate Sādhana (Spiritual Practice), and attuned to any of these subtle centres, one gets the corresponding cosmic experience, just as when we tune the radio to different wave-lengths, we get the programmes being broadcast from different places in the world on those wave-lengths.

Generally, the Sub-Suṣumnā-nāḍi, below the Mūlādhāra is also closed. If the Cosmic-Energy flows through it, then the demoniac nature in man will be intensely roused. He will be ṣatanic, full of lust and anger, and violent and destructive in nature. (See also Note No.1).

6. That is why we find babies everywhere use sounds like Amma, Mumma, etc, for mother. Hence Amma or Amba (b being a labial, like b in but) is the most universal natural sound or name for the 'Divine Mother' or Śakti (Divine Energy), the source of all phenomenal existence.

7. Given here are some triads that are, and can be identified with, the Mātras of Om and the

Ardha-mātrā or A-mātrā (Turīya) in A-U-M-...... for purposes of Upāsana. The list is not exhaustive. One may improvise according to the needs of one's Sādhana.

Object of Meditation	A	U	M	Turiya
Reality	Satyam	Jñānam	Anantam	Brahman/ Ātman
Reality	Sat	Cit	Ānanda	Brahman/ Ātman
Paramātman	Virāt	Hiraṇya garbha	Īśvara	Brahman/ Ātman
Jīvātman	Viśva	Taijasa	Prājña	Brahman/ Ātman
Trimūrti (Trinity) &	Brahmā	Viṣṇu	Śiva/ Rudra	Parame-śvara
Their Functions	Sṛṣti (Evolution of the Universe)	Sthiti (Protection of the Universe)	Praḷaya (Involution of the Universe)	Śāntam-Advaitam Non-dual Peace
Their Śaktis (Consorts)	Sarasvatī (Wisdom)	Lakṣmī (Wealth)	Pārvatī/ Kāli (Power)	Devi or Parameśvarī
Brahmāṇḍa (Universe)	Bhūḥ	Bhuvaḥ	Suvaḥ	Lokottara
Śarīra (Body)	Sthula (Gross)	Sūkṣma (Subtle)	Kāraṇa (Causal)	Bhāgavatī-tanu (Spiritual)

Šakti or Matrix	Prakṛtī	Avyakta	Māyā	Brahman/ Īśvara
Guṇas	Tamas	Rajas	Sattva	Triguṇātīta
Experience	Moha (Delusion)	Duhkha (Pain)	Sukha (Pleasure)	Ānanda (Bliss)
Framework of Universe	Space	Time	Causation	Transcendental Absolute
Time	Past	Present	Future	Absolute
State of Consciousness	Jāgrat (Waking)	Svapna (Dream)	Suṣupti (Deep-sleep)	Samādhi/ Turīya Super conscious Trance
Samsāra	Birth	Life	Death	Mukti/ Liberation
Vedas	Ṛk	Yajus	Sāma	Aum
Śabda (Sound)	Vaikharī	Madhyamā	Paśyantī	Parā

8. Even those who do not know the significance of Om, if they do its Japa with Śraddhā (Faith) in the prescribed manner, since Om is the Primordial Cosmic Sound, the Source of all words and thoughts, their minds will get attuned to It and be lifted up, just as a person is absorbed and lifted up by hearing good music, even if he does not know the science of music, nor can sing himself. Of course, the benefit is far greater if one does it with understanding (Cf. Gita, XIII.26).

9. Cf. Passage quoted from the Chāndogya Upaniṣad regarding the three Vyahṛtis. Later on the three Vyāhṛtis were raised to seven, by subdividing Suvaḥ into Suvaḥ, Mahaḥ, Janaḥ, Tapaḥ, and Satyam, corresponding to the seven higher worlds. These are used in the Mantras of the Sandhya-vandana and other rituals (Cf. the last para in the passage quoted from the Mahānārā-yaṇa Upaniṣad).

10. As already pointed out, the sound Om is produced by the combination of the three sounds, A, U, M. These are the three Mātras (Moras or phonetic components) of Om; further there is the Ardha-Mātrā (half-mora) of A-Mātrā, the inaudible sound which still lingers even when the audible sound dies away, and which can be detected only by fine perception and concentration.

Om being the sound-symbol of Brahman, it is considered to be the first vibration as sound emanating at the beginning of creation. From the three Mātras of Om came out the three 'feet' of Gāyatrī. And from its three 'feet' came out the three Vedas and the three Vyāhṛtis Bhūr-Bhuvaḥ-Suvaḥ, representing the three Cosmic World Planes. From A, came out '*Tat Savitur vareṇyam*', which expanded itself into the Ṛg-Veda and the Cosmic plane Bhūh; from U, '*Bhargo Devasya Dhīmahi*', which expanded itself into Yajur Veda and the plane of Bhuvaḥ; and from M, '*Dhiyo yo naḥ pracodayāt*', which expanded itself into Sāma-Veda, and the plane of Svaḥ. The first Veda is Stuti-para (devoted to Devotion), the second is Kriyā-para (devoted to Work), and the third is Jñāna-para (devoted to Knowledge).

So by the meditation upon the different Mātras different ends are attained according to the significations of the Mātras. But when the mind is concentrated upon the Ardha-mātrā, the Transcendental Brahman is realized.

Part II

Gāyatrī Mantra and the Sandhyā Upāsanā

I Sandhyā-Upasanā and Its Nature

In Part I, Section VII, we dealt with the importance of Om and the Gāyatrī-Mantra. [Om is Sabda-Brahman (the word Brahman or Logos), represented by the Vedas, and Gāyatrī-Mantra is considered the elaboration of Om and the spiritual 'Boon conferring Mother of the Vedas' (Varadā Veda-Mātā),[1] the Vedas being held as further elaboration of the Gāyatrī. Because of its supreme spiritual significance, the Gāyatrī-Mantra has been incorporated as the very core of a daily prayer-ritual known as Sandhyā][2] Being in the nature of contemplation, the ritual is classed as Upāsana or spiritual contemplation. This Upāsana is to be performed thrice a day at the conjunction (Sandhi) times of the night and dawn (Purvāhna), forenoon and afternoon (Madhyāhna) and evening (sunset) and night (Sāyāhna), lasting 48 minutes at each conjunction. If this is not possible under modern conditions it should be done in the morning and evening at least. As the Upāsanā is done at the conjunction-time (Sandhyā), it is designated as the Sandhyā-Upāsana. It is also called

Sandhyā-Vandana (adoration or worship), and often merely Sandhyā. It can be practised by all without distinction of caste, colour, creed or sex (cf. Sukla Yajur Veda XXVI 2)[3]

The sun above, the Giver of Life (Pūṣan) and Light (Tejas) (Cf. Īṣa Upaniṣad 16) is the great visible symbol of the Infinite Spiritual Sun, the source of all consciousness, the substratum of the entire Cosmic Universe, and the Inner Self (Antar-Ātman) of all entities and beings in all the worlds of the Cosmic Universe. Man is a part and parcel of this Cosmic Universe, and within the 'Supreme Space' (Parame-Vyoman) or 'Sky of his psychic Heart (Hridaya-Ākāśah) (Cf. Taittirīya Up., II 1.1; I.VI.1) is also indwelling that Spiritual Sun, reflected in the lake of his mind as the Jīva or Soul, which is the centre of individual consciousness. The Sandhyā-Upāsana, with the visible sun in the sky as the symbol, is a Sādhana (spiritual practice) to bring about the conjunction (Sandhi) of the individual Self with the Cosmic Self to realize the unity of both. Sandhyā, therefore, is a form of Yoga-Sādhana for the union of the individual with the Supreme Reality, and the Sandhyā-ritual incorporates the elements or features of all the four main types of Yoga — Karma, Bhakti, Dhyāna, and Jñāna.

Sandhyā is a specially devised efficient spiritual ritual for the realization of the Divinity of the Self (Ātman). It is therefore not a Kāmya Karma i.e. optional ritual to be performed occasionally for the attainment of worldly fulfilments. It is on the other hand a Nitya Karma or an obligatory daily ritual whose object is to bring about self-purification and attunement to Cosmic Reality. It is a wonderful mental exercise to elevate and equip the mind for this purpose. It is an all-round complete ritual which incorporates the principles of the Supreme Divinity (Brahman), Cosmic Creation, and Deities — Nature and Spirit and Spiritual Union or Liberation (Yoga or Moksa). As a result of its daily practice in the proper spirit, the mind is made pure, its present weaknesses and inertia are eliminated, and its inherent spiritual powers come into manifestation. The different aspects of the ritual are conducive to physical and mental health and vigour and psycho-somatic harmony. Thus Sandhyā is devised to lead to both physical and spiritual advancement (Abhyudaya and Niḥśreyasa).

II Rituals of the Sandhyā

In the elaboration of the Sandhyā-ritual this main purpose of spiritual elevation and the visualization of the union of the individual and the Universal is always kept in view. Those who are non-Advaitins can meditate on the love aspect of the personal deity and realise their kinship with Him as His eternal beloved devotees and servants. In the beginning, the mind is more impressed by concrete rituals than abstract thought. Hence ritualistic procedures are devised for the removal of the physical, mental, and psychic obstacles within to enable one to rise mentally step by step above the ego-centred life to the divine consciousness. Each part of the ritual is meant to give expression externally to an internal mental attitude and spiritual feeling (Bhāva). The main item, of course, is the repetition (Japa) of the Gāyatrī-Mantra and meditation on it, others coming in as auxiliaries. Appropriate Vedic Mantras are prescibed to be recited with these concrete ritualistic procedures for the purification of the mind and personality, and for generating the mental attitude helpful for concentration on Divine Truth. Some necessary changes are introduced in the Mantras and ritual according to the time of the Sandhyā—dawn, noon, or sunset, and according to the Veda (Ṛg, Yajur, or Sāma) to which the votary is affiliated. However, the main purpose as well as most of the Mantras, the procedures, and rituals are all common. In modern times, if one is not affiliated to any of the Vedas, he/she can adopt any one of them which can be conveniently learnt.

The procedures involve:

1. Ācamanam: Sipping a little water, in the prescribed manner, for self-purification, remembering the Supreme All-pervading Reality.

2. Āpo-Mārjanam: Invoking all the waters of the earth which form the cause of the emergence and sustenance of all life, by sprinkling water on oneself, to enable one to be attuned to the cosmic life and reality.

3. Prāṇāyāma: Regulated breathings, as per prescipition, for establishing psycho-somatic harmony, using the Gāyatrī-Mantra.

4. Punar-Ācamanam: Again sipping water with appropriate Mantras for the removal of all sins and obstacles, attuning oneself to the light-giving sun in the morning, to the life-giving waters at noon and to the heat-giving fire in the evening, which are the means of all our life and activity, and as such are termed as the sources of Immortality (Amṛta-yoni).

5. Punar-Mārjanam: Again sprinkling water over oneself with the Gāyatrī and other Mantras praying for welfare here in the world and highest spiritual attainment hereafter.

6. Aghāmarṣanam: Repeating the cosmic creation Mantras, feeling oneself as a part of it, to remove the limitations of personality.

7. Sūryopasthānam: Invoking the Sun-God who brings life and light to the world and attuning the mind to the Divine in the Sun and to all the cosmic surroundings.

8. Gāyatrī-Upāsanam: First the Divine Gāyatri is invoked as the source of the Vedas and then the different Worlds and the Supreme Divinity are located in the various limbs of one's body by touching them while uttering the Gāyatrī-Mantra, along with the Vyāhṛti (Bhuḥ, Bhuvaḥ, Svaḥ). This process of locating is known as Aṅga-Nyāsa. This is followed by the Japa and meditation of the Gāyatrī-Mantra for as long as one can do conveniently, fixing, however, a decent minimum number of times for the Japa. For meditation Gāyatri is conceived in the form of a luminous Goddess illuminating the Heart and removing all darkness of Ignorance.

9. Visarjanam: Valediction. Praying to the Goddess to retire, to return again when invoked. Salutations are offered with devotion.

10. Antya-prakaraṇāni: Ending. Now, concluding the Upāsana, protection against all wrongs and evils is sought and salutations are offered to the Sun-God and other Cosmic divinities. Forgiveness is sought for any flaws or lacunae in the uttering of the Mantras and the performance of the rituals and the Supreme Being is remembered to make them complete. The Upāsana is concluded with the offering of salutations.

III Preparation for the Performance of Sandhyā

Before performing the Sandhyā, one should be physically clean, mentally calm and restrained and have a prayerful attitude. One should sit in a clean quiet place on a grass-mat (Kuśāsana), or Deer-skin (Kṛṣṇājina) or a suitable cotton-carpet piece (or a combination of these where necessary), in a straight position (but not taut) with legs tucked in (ordinary Padmāsana). One must always keep in view that the purpose of the Sandhyā is the unification of the individual with the Universal at all levels. He should invoke the inner latent Divine Reality to be in harmony with the externally manifested Cosmic Reality. At the commencement of the Upāsana and at the end he must pray for the peace, happiness, and well being of all creatures, human and non-human.

The Mantras of the Sandhyā have to be learnt from a competent person with correct and clear pronunciation along with their meaning, to be mystically effective; for they are intended primarily to create an impression on one's own mind rather than to please the Deities outside. The Supreme Divinity is within oneself. 'Whatever one intensely thinks or meditates upon, that one becomes' is the psychological law (Yad-dhyāyati tad-bhavati). We see that even in ordinary life, if a speaker does not utter words properly and express the ideas clearly, one does not get the meaning and will therefore lose interest in it. Even the speaker himself feels dissatisfied.

The rituals, external and internal, must be performed punctiliously and artistically without clumsiness, in the proper prescibed manner, understanding their significance, uttering the Mantras clearly with earnestness (Niṣṭhā), faith (Śraddhā), and conviction (Viśvāsa), to yield greater results.

N O T E S

1. Mahānārayana Upanisad XXXVI 2: also XXXIV 1: "May the boon-conferring divine Gāyatri (Varadā Devī) come to us (in order to instruct us about)

the Imperishable Brahman who is revealed by the Vedas. May Gāyatrī the Mother of Metres (Mantras) (*Chandasām-Mātā*), favour us with the knowledge of the Supreme Brahman alluded to."

2. Śrī Rāmakṛṣṇa used to say that the Sandhyā merges in the Gāyatri, and the Gāyatri merges in Om.

3. In the present times, if one is unable to do the Sandhyā-Upāsana thrice a day, the mid-day Sandhya can be omitted. At least once a day in the morning or evening it should be done. When one is really very busy with work, and not as an excuse, one may on those days adopt a shorter form keeping the essentials intact. A solitary place is the best for the performance of Sandhyā.

Though in regard to the Śūdras (labouring class) and women the Sandhya was not prescribed in later times due to various social circumstances, it was permissible to all in earlier Vedic times. In the Śukla Yajur Vedas (XXVI-2) it is urged to spread the beneficent words (*Vācām kalyāṇīm*) of the Vedas to all the people without distinction of caste, creed, or sex, even to people of other religions.

"Yathā-imām vācam kalyaṇīm ādadāmi (avadāmi) janebhyaḥ;

Brahma-rājanyābhyām Śūdrāya ca āryāya ca svāya-cāraṇāya ca (Just as I am speaking these blessed words to the people (without distinction), in the same way you also spread these words among all men and women — the Brāhmaṇas, Kṣatriyas, Vaiśyas, Sudrās and all other, whether they be our own people or aliens.) ['Quoted by Swami Vivekananda in his speech 'The Religion we are Born In' - Complete Works, Vol. III. p.457].

Now the time has come, as declared by Swami Vivekananda, that the Vedas and the Gāyatrī Mantra must be propagated among all as before, irrespective of caste, creed, sex or religion.

Women also should perform Sandhyā as in olden times. As it has been said in one of the Smṛtis:

Purā-kalpe kumārīṇām
maunjī-bandhanam-īhyate
Adhyāpanam ca vedānām sāvitrī-vacanam tathā.

(In olden times the Upanayana was performed for the girls too. They were taught the Vedas and the Gāyatrī Mantra (Manusmṛti: Prathama Pariśiṣṭa 13:14). We see in the Rāmāyaṇa Sītā performing the Sandhyā.

4. In the Īśa Upaniṣad, verse 15, the Sādhaka (Spiritual aspirant) prays, "Like a golden disc, Thy shining orb covers the Face of Truth. Remove it, O Sun, so that I who am devoted to virtue and Truth may behold it." In the next verse, continuing the prayer, he affirms the identity of the Self within him with the Universal Self manifested through the Sun: "O Sun, the offspring of Prajāpati (the Lord of Beings), Thou lonely courser of the heavens, Thou controller and supporter of all, contract Thy dazzling rays. With Thy grace, may I behold the most blessed and luminous form of Thine. I am indeed He, that Supreme Being who dwells there in Thee (*Yosāvasau puruṣaḥ soham asmi*).

Cf. Svetāśvatara Upaniṣad (VI.11); "The One Effulgent Divinity is hidden in all beings. He is all-pervading, and is the Inner Self of all creatures. He presides over all actions, and all beings reside in Him. He is the Inner-witness (Sākṣī). He endows all with consciousness (Cetā), and He is the Absolute (Kevalaḥ), free from the three Guṇas (characteristics) of Nature (Nirguṇa).

Part III
Details of the Practice of Sandhyā Worship

For the convenience of those who intend to use the book for the performance of Sandhya in the orthodox style, a part III has been added which gives complete details regarding the mantras to be chanted and the procedures to be adopted. It is however essential that in the midst of attending to all the details, the essence of the Sandhya-Vandana, namely, the repetition of the Gayatri-mantra with contemplation of its meaning, should not be forgotten. Also it is specially warned that the practice of Pranayama should not be done by those who have any heart trouble. Holding the breath in and out are detrimental to those who have not perfect health.

1. आचमनम् || *Ācamanam*

Sipping water sanctified by mantras.

Sit in a squatting position, facing east or north. The hands should be between the knees. Bend all the fingers other than the thumb and the small finger slightly so that a hollow is produced in the palm. Take a very small quantity of water in the palm and sip, uttering the following three mantras (one sip for each mantra):-

अच्युताय नमः । *Acyutāya namaḥ*

अनन्ताय नमः । *Anantāya namaḥ*

गोविन्दाय नमः । *Govindāya namaḥ*

Then utter केशव *Keśava* and नारायण *Narāyaṇa* touching the right cheek and the left cheek respectively with the thumb of the right hand.

Utter माधव *Mādhava* and गोविन्द *Govinda*, touching the right eye and the left eye respectively with the ring finger.

Utter विष्णो *Viṣṇo* and मधुसूदन *Madhusūdana*, touching the right nostril and the left nostril respectively with the index finger.

Utter त्रिविक्रम *Trivikrama* and वामन *Vāmana*, touching the right ear and the left ear respectively with the small finger.

Utter श्रीधर *Śrīdhara* and हृषीकेश *Hṛṣīkeśa*, touching the right shoulder and the left shoulder respectively with the middle finger.

Utter पद्मनाभ *Padmanābha* and दामोदर *Dāmodara* touching the navel and the head respectively with all the fingers.

By these actions the various parts of the body are sanctified and the person is made fit to proceed with the worship.

2. विघ्नेश्वरध्यानम्।। *Vighneśvara Dhyānam*

Meditation on Lord *Vighneśvara*

While reciting the following mantra, gently tap the two sides of the forehead with the fists five times with the thought that thereby the nectar (*amṛta*) in the head flows down through all the nerves and invigorates them.

शुक्लाम्बरधरं विष्णुं शशिवर्णं चतुर्भुजम् ।
प्रसन्नवदनं ध्यायेत् सर्वविघ्नोपशान्तये ।।

Śuklāmbaradharam Viṣṇum
śaśivarṇam caturbhujam,
Prasannavadanam dhyāyet
sarva-vighnopaśāntaye.

For the removal of all obstacles I meditate on Lord *Vighneśvara* who is clad in white, is all-pervading, is white like the moon, sports four arms and is always of serene aspect.

3. प्राणायाम: *Prāṇāyāmaḥ*

Regulation of breath.

Bend the index finger and the middle finger and press the right nostril with the thumb and left nostril with the ring finger and the small finger. First draw in the breath through the left nostril while mentally chanting the following mantra. Then hold the breath within, mentally chanting the same mantra again. Thereafter, let the breath out through the right nostril, again mentally chanting the same mantra. These three actions of inhaling, holding the breath and exhaling, during which the mantra is chanted three times, together make up one *Prāṇāyāmaḥ*.

ओं भूः । ओं भुवः । ओं सुवः । ओं महः ।
ओं जनः । ओं तपः । ओं सत्यम् ॥
ओं तत् सवितुर्वरेण्यं
भर्गो देवस्य धीमहि ।
धियो यो नः प्रचोदयात् ॥
ओमापो ज्योती रसोऽमृतं ब्रह्म भूर्भुवस्सुवरोम् ॥

Om Bhūḥ, Om Bhuvaḥ, Om Suvaḥ, Om Mahaḥ
Om Janaḥ, Om Tapaḥ, Om Satyam.
Om Tat Saviturvareṇyam

Bhargo devasya dhīmahi,
Dhiyo yo naḥ procodayāt.
Om āpo jyotī raso amṛtam brahma
Bhūr Bhuvas suvar om.

Om is all the lokas— *bhūḥ, bhuvaḥ, suvaḥ, mahaḥ, janaḥ, tapaḥ, satyam.*

We meditate on the adorable effulgence of the Lord who creates everything, so that it may energize our consciousness.

Om is water, light, the earth that yields tasty food, the air that sustains life, the all-pervading ether and the mind, intellect and the 'I' sense marked by the terms bhūḥ, bhuvaḥ and suvaḥ.

4. संकल्पः || *Saṅkalpaḥ*

Resolution

Place the left palm, turned upward, on the right thigh and place the right palm, turned downward on the left palm. Recite the following mantra:

ममोपात्त-समस्त-दुरित-क्षय-द्वारा-श्री परमेश्वर-प्रीत्यर्थं—

Mamopātta samasta durita kṣaya dvārā śrī parameśvara prītyartham—

In the morning -

प्रातः सन्ध्यां उपासिष्ये -

Prātaḥ sandhyām upāsiṣye -

At noon -

माध्याह्निकं करिष्ये -

Mādhyāhnikam kariṣye -

In the evening -

सायं सन्ध्यां उपासिष्ये -

Sāyam sandhyām upāsiṣye -

I begin to worship the goddess of *sandhya* in the morning (at noon/in the evening) in order to merit God's grace which destroys all the sins acquired by me.

5. मार्जनम् || *Mārjanam*

Purification of the body and mind.

Uttering ओं केशवाय नमः *Om Keśavāya namaḥ*, write ओं *Om* on water with the ring finger and touch the spot between the two eyebrows with that finger.

Then, while reciting the first seven of the following nine mantras, sprinkle water on the head with the ring finger. While reciting the eighth mantra, sprinkle water on the feet. Again sprinkle water on the head while reciting the ninth mantra.

आपो हि ष्ठा मयो भुवः ।

Āpo hi ṣṭhā mayo bhuvaḥ.

ता न ऊर्जे दधातन ।

Tā na ūrje dadhātana.

महे रणाय चक्षसे ।

Mahe raṇāya cakṣase.

यो वः शिवतमो रसः ।

Yo vaḥ śivatamo rasaḥ.

तस्य भाजयतेह नः ।

Tasya bhājayateha naḥ.

उशतीरिव मातरः ।

Uśatīriva mātaraḥ.

तस्मा अरं गमाम वः ।

Tasmā aram gamāma vaḥ.

यस्य क्षयाय जिन्वथ ।

Yasya kṣayāya jinvatha.

आपो जनयथा च नः ।

Āpo janayathā ca naḥ.

Now take a little water in the palm and rotate the palm around the head with the following mantra:

ओं भूर्भुवः सुवः ॥

Om Bhūr bhuvaḥ suvaḥ.

It is well-known that you, the deities of water, are the cause of great happiness. Please nourish us with the divine vision which brings glory and loveliness. Please make us worthy of imbibing the auspicious bliss even as a mother feeds her children. We approach you with eagerness for that bliss to distribute which you have taken a form and are shining. Bestow on us the boon of a next life sanctified by knowledge.

6. प्राशनम् ॥ *Prāśanam*

Sipping water with mantra

Take a little water in the palm and sip, after reciting the following mantra.

(प्रातः) सूर्यश्च मा मन्युश्च मन्युपतयश्च मन्युकृतेभ्यः । पापेभ्यो रक्षन्ताम् । यद्रात्र्या पापमकार्षम् । मनसा वाचा हस्ताभ्याम् ।

पद्भ्यामुदरेण शिश्ना । रात्रि-स्तदवलुंपतु । यत्किंच दुरितं मयि । इदमहं माममृत-योनौ । सूर्ये ज्योतिषि जुहोमि स्वाहा ॥

(Prātaḥ) Sūryaśca mā manyuśca manyupatayaśca manyukṛtebhyaḥ. Pāpebhyo rakṣantām. Yadrātryā pāpamakārṣam. Manasā vācā hastābhyām. padbhyām udareṇa śiśnā. Rātris-tadavalumpatu. Yatkiñca duritam mayi. Idam aham māmamṛta yonau. Sūrye jyotiṣi juhomi svāhā.

(In the morning) May the sun who stimulates everything, anger which enslaves all and the gods who preside over anger, protect me from the sins committed through anger. May the deity of the night absolve me of the sins committed by me at night with the mind, lips, hands, legs, stomach as also of whatever other sins may linger in me. This "me" devoid of all sins, I offer as sacrifice in the effulgence of the sun who is the source of immortality. May this sacrifice be well done.

(मध्याह्ने) आपः पुनन्तु पृथिवीं पृथिवी पूता पुनातु माम् । पुनन्तु ब्रह्मण-स्पति-र्ब्रह्म-पूता पुनातु माम् । यदुच्छिष्ट-मभोज्यं यद्वा दुश्चरितं मम । सर्वं पुनन्तु मामा-पोऽसतां च प्रतिग्रहँ स्वाहा ॥

(Madhyāhne) Āpaḥ punantu pṛthivīm pṛthivī pūtā panātu mām. punantu brahmaṇas-

patirbrahma-pūtā punātu mām. Yaducchiṣṭam-abhojyam yadvā duścaritam mama. Sarvam punantu māmāpo asatām ca pratigraham svāhā.

(At noon) May the deity of water sanctify the earth which is its base. May the sanctified earth purify me. May it sanctify the teacher who is the channel for the Veda. May the ever pure Veda purify me. May the deity of water absolve me from sins incurred through consuming food left by others or food unfit to be eaten, through bad contact and through receiving gifts from the wicked. Thus purified I offer myself as sacrifice in the Supreme effulgence.

(सायंकाले) अग्निश्च मा मन्युश्च मन्यु पतयश्च मन्युकृतेभ्यः पापेभ्यो रक्षन्ताम् । यदह्ना पापमकार्षम् । मनसा वाचा हस्ताभ्याम् । पद्भ्यामुदरेण शिश्ना । अहस्तदवलुंपतु । यत्किंच दुरितं मयि । इदमहं माममृतयोनौ । सत्ये ज्योतिषि जुहोमि स्वाहा ॥

(Sāyankāle) Agniśca mā manyuśca manyupatayaśca manyukṛtebhyaḥ. Pāpebhyo rakṣantām. Yadahnā pāpamakārṣam. Manasā vācā hastābhyām. Padbhyām udareṇa śiśnā.

Ahastadavalumpatu. Yatkiñca duritam mayi. Idam aham māmamṛta yonau. Satye jyotiṣi juhomi svāhā.

(In the evening) May the Fire who stimulates everything, anger which enslaves all and the gods who preside over anger, protect me from the sins committed through anger. May the deity of the day absolve me of the sins committed by me at day-time with the mind, lips, hands, legs, stomach as also of whatever sins lingering in me. This "me" devoid of sins, I offer as sacrifice in the effulgence of Truth who is the source of immortality. May this sacrifice be well done.

7. पुनर्मार्जनम् । *Punarmārjanam*

Sprinkling water again.

Sprinkle water on the head with the following mantra:

दधिक्राव्ण्णो अकारिषम् । जिष्णोरश्वस्य वाजिनः । सुरभि नो मुखाकरत् । प्रण आयूँषि तारिषत् ।

Dadhikrāvṇṇo akāriṣam. Jiṣṇoraśvasya vājinaḥ. Surabhi no mukhākarat. Praṇa āyūṁṣi tāriṣat.

आपो हि ष्ठा etc as in No.5 above.
Āpo hi ṣṭhā etc as in No.5 above.

End with ओं भूर्भुवःसुवः *Om Bhūrbhuvaḥ suvaḥ*

I make obeisance to the Supreme Person who supports, rules and sustains all the worlds, who is ever victorious and who has taken the form of *Hayagrīva* the repository of all knowledge. May He make our faces and other organs fragrant. May He protect our lives continuously. It is well-known... knowledge (as in No.5 above).

8. अर्घ्य-प्रदानम् || *Arghya-pradānam*

Offering water.

Morning:

Stand facing east. Take plenty of water in both palms and, raising the heels a little, pour the water down through the tips of the fingers other than the thumb uttering the following mantra. This is to be done three times.

ओं भूर्भुवस्सुवः। तत् सवितुर्वरेण्यं भर्गो देवस्य धीमहि । धियो यो नः प्रचोदयात् ॥

Om Bhūrbhuvassuvaḥ. Tat saviturvareṇyam bhargo devasya dhīmahi. Dhiyo yo naḥ pracodayāt.

[Meaning - see No.3 - We meditate ... consciousness]

Noon:
Stand facing north and do the same twice.

Evening:
Squat facing west and do the same three times.

9. प्रायश्चित्तार्घ्यम् || *Prāyaścittārghyam*

Offering of water in atonement for failure to perform the worship at the proper time.

Do *Prāṇāyāmaḥ* once, as in No.3. Thereafter offer *arghya* once, as in No.8. Then uttering ओं भूर्भुवस्सुवः *Om Bhūrbhuvas suvaḥ* turn round once and sprinkle a little water around you.

10. ऐक्यानुसन्धानम् || *Aikyānusandhānam*

Meditation on the identity of the individual self and the Supreme Self.

Sit down, close the eyes and mentally chant:

असावादित्यो ब्रह्म । ब्रह्मैवाहमस्मि ||

Asāvādityo brahma. Brahmaivāhamasmi.

This sun is Brahman. I too am Brahman.

Do *ācamanam* once, as in No.1.

11. देव-तर्पणम् || *Deva-Tarpaṇam*

Offering of water to the devas.

Morning: Squat, facing east.
Noon: Squat, facing north.
Evening: Squat, facing north.

Pour water through the finger tips of both hands reciting the following mantras:

आदित्यं तर्पयामि	*Ādityam tarpayāmi*
सोमं तर्पयामि	*Somam tarpayāmi*
अंगारकं तर्पयामि	*Aṅgārakam tarpayāmi*
बुधं तर्पयामि	*Budham tarpayāmi*
बृहस्पतिं तर्पयामि	*Bṛhaspatim tarpayāmi*
शुक्रं तर्पयामि	*Śukram tarpayāmi*
शनैश्चरं तर्पयामि	*Śanaiścaram tarpayāmi*
राहुं तर्पयामि	*Rāhum tarpayāmi*
केतुं तर्पयामि	*Ketum tarpayāmi*
केशवं तर्पयामि	*Keśavam tarpayāmi*

नारायणं तर्पयामि	*Nārāyaṇam tarpayāmi*
माधवं तर्पयामि	*Mādhavam tarpayāmi*
गोविन्दं तर्पयामि	*Govindam tarpayāmi*
विष्णुं तर्पयामि	*Viṣṇum tarpayāmi*
मधुसूदनं तर्पयामि	*Madhusūdanam tarpayāmi*
त्रिविक्रमं तर्पयामि	*Trivikramam tarpayāmi*
वामनं तर्पयामि	*Vāmanam tarpayāmi*
श्रीधरं तर्पयामि	*Śrīdharam tarpayāmi*
हृषीकेशं तर्पयामि	*Hṛṣīkeśam tarpayāmi*
पद्मनाभं तर्पयामि	*Padmanābham tarpayāmı*
दामोदरं तर्पयामि	*Dāmodaram tarpayāmi*

I make my offering to the presiding deities of the nine planets — *Āditya, Soma, Aṅgāraka, Budha, Bṛhaspati, Śukra, Śani* (who moves slowly), *Rāhu,* and *Ketu*; and *Nārāyaṇa* with twelve names — *Keśava, Nārāyaṇa, Mādhava, Govinda, Viṣṇu, Madhusūdana, Trivikrama, Vāmana, Śrīdhara, Hṛṣīkeśa, Padmanābha, Dāmodara.*

Do *ācamanam* once, as in No.1.

12. जपसंकल्पः || *Japasaṅkalpaḥ*

Sankalpa for Japa.

Sit on a wooden plank or small carpet. The eyes should be half-closed and the mind should be concentrated on the mantras which are to be uttered mentally.

Morning: Sit facing east
Noon: Sit facing north
Evening: Sit facing west

The vessel of water should be kept in front. First chant,

शुक्लाम्बरधरं... विघ्नोपशान्तये ।
ओं भूर्भुवस्सुवरोम् ॥

Śuklāmbaradharam... Vighnopaśāntaye (as in No.2) *Om Bhūrbhuvassuvarom*

Then do one *prāṇāyāmaḥ*

Now chant the following, with the palms as in No.4

ममोपात्तसमस्तदुरितक्षयद्वारा श्री परमेश्वर प्रीत्यर्थं -

Mamopātta samasta duritakṣayadvārā śri parameśvara prītyartham —

Morning: प्रातः सन्ध्या गायत्रीमहामन्त्रजपं करिष्ये ।

Prātah sandhyā gāyatrī mahāmantra japam kariṣye.

Noon: माध्याह्निक गायत्रीमहामन्त्रजपं करिष्ये ।

Mādhyāhnika gāyatrīmahāmantra japam kariṣye.

Evening: सायं सन्ध्या गायत्रीमहामन्त्रजपं करिष्ये ।

Sāyam sandhyā gāyatrīmahāmantra japam kariṣye.

I start performing the great mantra of *gāyatri* in the morning (noon/evening) in order to get the grace of God by removing all the sins incurred by me.

13. प्रणवजपः || *Prañava-japaḥ*

Japa of *Praṇavaḥ*

Touching the head with the fingers of the right hand, recite

प्रणवस्य ऋषिः ब्रह्मा ।

Praṇavasya.ṛṣiḥ brahmā.

Touching the upper lip, recite

देवी गायत्री छन्दः ।

Devī gāyatrī chandaḥ

Touching the chest, recite

परमात्मा देवता ।

Paramātmā devatā.

Again touching the head, recite

भूरादि सप्त व्याहृतीनां अत्रि भृगु कुत्स वसिष्ठ गौतम काश्यपाङ्गिरस ऋषयः ।

Bhūrādi sapta vyāhṛtīnām atri bhṛgu kutsa vasiṣṭha gautama kāśyapāṅgirasa ṛṣayaḥ.

Touching the upper lip, recite

गायत्री उष्णिक् अनुष्टुप् बृहती पङ्क्ती तृष्टुप् जगत्यः छन्दांसि ।

Gāyatrī uṣṇik anuṣṭup bṛhatī paṅktī tṛṣṭup jagatyaḥ chandāmsi.

Touching the chest, recite

अग्नि वायु अर्क वागीश वरुण इन्द्र विश्वेदेवा देवताः ।

Agni vāyu arka vāgīśa varuṇa indra viśvedevā devatāḥ.

Now do ten prāṇāyāmas as in No.3.

For Omkāra, *Ṛṣi* is *Brahmā*; *chandas* is *Devī gāyatrī*, deity is *Paramātman*.

For the seven *vyāhṛtis* commencing from *Bhūḥ*, the *ṛṣis* are *Atri, Bhṛgu, Kutsa, Vasiṣṭha, Gautama, Kāśyapa* and *Āṅgirasa*.

The *chandas* are *gāyatri, uṣṇik, anuṣṭup, bṛhatī, paṅktī, tṛṣṭup* and *jagatī*.

The deities are Agni, Vāyu, Arka, Vāgīśa, Varuṇa, Indra, and *Viśvedevāḥ*.

Then do three Prāṇāyāmas repeating the mantra (as in section 3) thrice for each Prāṇāyāma — thus chanting the mantra nine times.

14. गायत्री आवाहनम् || *Gāyatrī-āvāhanam*

Invoking *Gāyatrī devi*

Touching the head, recite

आयातु इति अनुवाकस्य वामदेव ऋषिः

Āyātu iti anuvākasya vāmadeva ṛṣiḥ.

Touching the upper lip, recite

अनुष्टुप् छन्दः ।

Anuṣṭup chandaḥ

Touching the chest, recite

गायत्री देवता ।

Gāyatrī devatā

With the following mantras invoke *gāyatrī devī* in the heart by means of the *Āvāhanī mudra* (to be learnt from the teacher)

आयातु वरदा देवी अक्षरं ब्रह्मसंमितम् ।
गायत्री छन्तसां मातेदं ब्रह्म जुषस्व नः ॥
ओजोऽसि सहोऽसि बलमसि भ्राजोऽसि
देवानां धामनामासि विश्वमसि विश्वायुः
सर्वमसि सर्वायुरभिभूरों
गायत्रीमावाहयामि सावित्रीमावाहयामि
सरस्वतीमावाहयामि.

Āyātu varadā devī akṣaram brahma sammitam.
Gāyatrī chandasām mātedam brahma juṣasva naḥ.
Ojo'si saho'si balamasi bhrājo'si devānām dhāmanāmāsi viśvamasi viśvāyus sarvamasi sarvāyurabhibhūrom gāyatrīmāvāhayāmi savitrīmāvāhayāmi sarasvatīmāvāhayāmi.

For the *anuvāka āyātu* the *ṛsi* is *Vāmadeva, chandas anuṣṭup* and deity *gāyatrī.*

May gāyatrī devī who bestows all the boons we seek, who is eternal, who is to be known through the Vedas and who is the Mother of the Vedas, appear here and now and accept this hymn of Vedic praise.

Gāyatri, You are the vital force, the power of the sense organs, you quell enemies; You are superbly healthy in your limbs; You are the light of knowledge; You are the famous effulgence of the celestials; You are the cosmos; You are the life of the world marked by time; You are everything; You are the life of all; You transcend everything.

Then, touching the head, recite

सावित्र्या ऋषिः विश्वामित्रः ।

Sāvitryā ṛsiḥ viśvāmitraḥ

Touching the upper lip, recite

निचृद्गायत्री छन्दः ।

Nicṛdgāyatrī chandaḥ

Touching the chest, recite

सविता देवता ।

Savitā devatā.

For the *gāyatrī* mantra, the *ṛsi* is *viśvāmitra, chandas nicṛdgāyatrī* and the deity *Savitā.*

15. गायत्रीजपः || *Gāyatrī japaḥ*

Gayatri japa

Morning: Stand facing east, the palms joined and held in front of your face.

Noon: Stand or sit facing east, the joined palms in front of the chest.

Evening: Sit facing west, the joined palms in front of your navel.

The hands should be covered with the *Aṅgavastra*. The mantra should be chanted mentally without movement of the lips. After each of the following lines you should pause for a second. There will thus be a total of five pauses. The mind should be concentrated on the meaning of the mantra.

ओम् ।

Om

भूर्भुवस्सुवः ।

Bhūrbhuvas suvaḥ

तत्सवितुर्वरेण्यम् ।

Tat savitur vareṇyam

भर्गो देवस्य धीमहि ।

Bhargo devasya dhīmahi

धियो यो नः प्रचोदयात् ।

Dhiyo yo naḥ pracodayāt

[Meaning: see No.3 - We meditate... consciousness]

This gayatri should be chanted 108 times. If there is not enough time, chant at least 54 or 28 times. But make up the deficit when you get time.

16. गायत्री उपस्थानम् ।। *Gāyatrī upasthānam*

Prayer to *gāyatrī* to return to Her abode.

First do *prāṇāyāma* once, sitting down.

Then stand up, facing the same direction as in No.15, join the palms and recite:

Morning: प्रातः सन्ध्या उपस्थानं करिष्ये ।

Prātaḥ sandhyā upasthānam kariṣye.

उत्तमे शिखरे देवी भूम्यां पर्वत मूर्धनि । ब्राह्मणेभ्यो ह्यनुज्ञानं गच्छ देवि यथा सुखम् ।।

Uttame śikhare devī bhūmyām parvata mūrdhani. Brāhmaṇebhyo hyanujñānam gaccha devi yathāsukham.

Noon: आदित्योपस्थानं करिष्ये ।

Ādityopasthānam kariṣye.

उत्तमे... सुखम् ।

uttame... sukham.

Evening: सायं सन्ध्योपस्थानं करिष्ये ।

Sāyam sandhyopasthānam kariṣye.

उत्तमे... सुखम् ।

uttame... sukham.

Praising the *gāyatrī devī* I pray to Her to return to Her abode, in the morning. (At noon I do *Ādityopasthāna* /In the evening I do *sāyam sandhyopasthāna*)

O radiant *gāyatrī* bless us on earth who are worshipping Brahman. Please return joyously to your divine abode on the highest pinnacle of Mount Meru.

17. सूर्योपस्थानम् ॥ *Sūryopasthānam*

Worship of the Sun-god.

Stand facing the same direction in which the japa is done, join the palms and salute the Paramatman who is shining in the centre of the rising sun.

Morning: मित्रस्य चर्षणी धृतः श्रवो देवस्य सानसिम् । सत्यं चित्रश्रवस्तमम् ॥
मित्रो जनान् यातयति प्रजानन् मित्रो दाधार पृथिवीमुतद्याम् । मित्रः कृष्टीरनिमिषाभिचष्टे सत्याय हव्यं घृतवद्विधेम ॥
प्र स मित्र मर्तो अस्तु प्रयस्वान् यस्त आदित्य शिक्षति व्रतेन । न हन्यते न जीयते त्वोतो नेनमँहो अश्नोत्यन्तितो न दूरात् ॥

Mitrasya carṣaṇī dhṛtaḥ śravo devasya sānasim. Satyam citraśravastamam.
Mitro janān yātayati prajānan mitro dādhāra pṛthivīmutadyām. Mitraḥ kṛṣṭīranimiṣābhicaṣṭhe satyāya havyam ghṛtavadvidhema.
Pra sa mitra marto astu prayasvān yasta āditya śikṣati vratena. Na hanyate na jīyate tvoto nenamamho aśnotyantito na dūrāt.

I meditate on the glory and fame of the all-protecting sun which is adorable, eternal, bewitching the hearts of all listeners.

The sun guides all, knowing everything. He supports the earth and the sky. He watches all creation unwinkingly. To Him we offer cooked rice soaked in ghee for attaining eternal fruits.

O sun who is Mitra, may he who longs to worship You scrupulously get the full benefit of righteousness.

One protected by you will not suffer from any disease; sin will not approach him from far or near.

Noon: आसत्येन रजसा वर्तमानो निवेशयन्नमृतं मर्त्यं च ।
हिरण्ययेन सविता रथेनाऽऽदेवो याति भुवना विपश्यन् ॥
उद्वयं तमसस्परि पश्यन्तो ज्योतिरुत्तरम् । देवं देवत्रा सूर्यमगन्म ज्योतिरुत्तमम् । उदुत्यं जातवेदसं देवं वहन्ति केतवः । दृशे विश्वाय सूर्यम् ॥
चित्रं देवानामुदगादनीकं चक्षुर्मित्रस्य वरुणस्याग्नेः । आ प्रा द्यावा पृथिवी अन्तरिक्षँ सूर्य आत्मा जगतस्तस्थुषश्च । तच्चक्षुर्देवहितं पुरस्ताच्छुक्रमुच्चरत् ॥
पश्येम शरदश्शतं, जीवेम शरदश्शतं, नन्दाम शरदश्शतं, मोदाम शरदश्शतं, भवाम शरदश्शतँ शृणवाम शरदश्शतं, प्रब्रवाम शरदश्शतमजीतास्याम शरदश्शतं ज्योक् च सूर्यंदृशे ॥
य उदगान्महतोऽर्णवाद्विभ्राजमानः सरिरस्य मध्यात् समा वृषभो लोहिताक्षस्सूर्यो विपश्चिन् मनसा पुनातु ॥

Āsatyena rajasā vartamāno niveśayannamṛtam martyam ca. Hiraṇyayena savitā rathenādevo yāti bhuvanā vipaśyan.

Udvayam tamasaspari paśyanto jyotiruttaram. Devam devatrā sūryamaganma jyotiruttamam. Udutyam jātavedasam devam vahanti ketavaḥ. Dṛśe viśvāya sūryam.

Citram devānāmudagādanīkam cakṣurmitrasya varuṇasyāgneḥ. Ā prā dyāvā pṛthivī antarikṣam sūrya ātmā jagatastasthuṣaśca. Taccakṣurdevahitam purastācchukramuccarat.

Paśyema śaradaśśatam, jīvema śaradaśśatam, nandāma śaradaśśatam, modāma śaradaśśatam, bhavāma śaradaśśatam, śṛṇavāma śaradaśśatam, prabravāma śaradaśśatam, ajītāsyāma śaradaśśatam jyok ca sūryandṛśe.

Ya udagānmahato arṇavādvibhrājamānaḥ sarirasya madhyāt samā vṛṣabho lohitākṣassūryo vipaścin manasā punātu.

The Sun riding a golden chariot goes round scrutinizing all the worlds and shining with self-effulgence and directing by means of His radiance celestials and humans in their respective tasks. The Sun rises swallowing darkness, with great splendour, protecting the celestials also. We who gaze at the Sun shall attain the great radiance of the Self.

For inspecting the worlds the horses of the Sun in the form of His rays bear Him, the god who knows everything.

Up rises the Sun who is like an eye to *Mitraḥ Varuṇaḥ* and *Agniḥ* and who is of the form of all the celestials. He the Lord of all moving and unmoving things pervades the heavens, the earth and the middle regions.

May we see and adore for a hundred years that orb of the Sun which rises in the east and looks after the welfare of the celestials like an eye. May we live thus for a hundred years. May we rejoice with our kith and kin for a hundred years. May we live gloriously for a hundred years. May we speak sweetly for a hundred years. May we live for a hundred years undefeated by the forces of evil. We desire to enjoy gazing at the Sun for a hundred years.

May my whole mind be sanctified by the Sun who bestows all our needs, whose eyes are red, who is omniscient and who rises from amidst the waters of the ocean illumining all the quarters.

Evening: इमं मे वरुण श्रुधी हवमद्या च मृडय ।
त्वामवस्युराचके ॥

तत्त्वा यामि ब्रह्मणा वन्दमानस्तदाशास्ते यजमानो हविर्भिः ।
अहेडमानो वरुणेह बोध्युरुशँ स मा न आयुः प्रमोषीः ॥

यच्चिद्धिते विशो यथा प्रदेव वरुण व्रतम् । मिनीमसि द्यवि द्यवि ॥
यत्किंचेदं वरुण दैव्ये जनेऽभिद्रोहं मनुष्याश्चरामसि ।
अचित्तीयत्तव धर्मा युयोपिम मा नस्तस्मादेनसो देव रीरिषः ॥

कितवासो यद्रिरिपुर्न दीवि यद्वाघ सत्यमुत यन्न विद्म । सर्वा ता विष्य शिथिरेव देवाथा ते स्याम वरुण प्रियासः ॥

Imam me varuṇa śrudhī havamadyā ca mṛḍaya. Tvāmavasyurācake.

Tattvā yāmi brahmaṇā vandamānastadāśāste yajamano havirbhiḥ. Aheḍamāno varuṇeha bodhyuruśam sa mā na āyuḥ pramoṣīh.

Yacciddhite viśo yathā pradeva varuṇa vratam. Minīmasi dyavi dyavi.

Yatkiñcedam varuṇa daivye jane abhidroham manuṣyāścarāmasi. Acittīyattava dharmā yuyopima mā nastasmādenaso deva rīriṣaḥ.

Kitavāso yadriripurna dīvi yadvāghā satyamuta yanna vidma. sarvā tā viṣya śithireva devāthā te syāma varuṇa priyāsaḥ.

O Varuṇa, please fulfil this prayer of mine and make me happy here and now. I pray for Thy protection.

I seek refuge in Thee uttering the Vedic mantras. The sacrificers seek Thee with the ingredients of offering.

O famous Varuṇa, please accept my prayer and don't ignore it. Please do not shorten my span of life.

O Lord Varuṇa, please protect us without punishing us for sins committed by us in different ways — by omitting to perform daily Thy worship like the ignorant folk, by committing frauds on the celestials because of human ignorance or by infringing the path of righteousness laid down by you.

O Varuṇa, please expunge the sin like those attributed to me unjustly by wicked people like gamblers who go where the good do not go or the sins committed by me consciously or unconsciously. We must ever remain beloved of you.

18. समष्ट्यभिवादनम् ।। *Samaṣṭyabhivādanam*

Prostration to all.

Stand facing the same direction as in No.17. Turn round to the next direction after each of the first four mantras. Then stand facing the original direction for the remaining mantras, palms joined.

सन्ध्यायै नमः, सावित्र्यै नमः । गायत्र्यै नमः । सरस्वत्यै नमः । सर्वाभ्यो देवताभ्यो नमो नमः ।। कामोऽकार्षीन्मन्युरकार्षीत् नमो नमः ।।

Sandhyāyai namaḥ. Sāvitryai namaḥ. Gāyatryai namaḥ. Sarasvatyai namaḥ. Sarvābhyo devatābhyo namo namaḥ. Kāmo akārṣīt manyurakārṣīt namo namaḥ.

Salutations to goddessess *Sandhyā, Sāvitrī, Gāyatrī, Sarasvatī* and all the deities. The sins I committed were impelled by desire and anger and not of my own free will. The sins that arose out of ignorance under the compulsion of desire must all be forgiven. O gods, I bow to you again and again.

Now cover both the ears with the fingers of the two hands and recite the following, touching the ground at the end with the hands. (The *Ṛṣis* etc, vary for each *gotraḥ* and are therefore to be learnt from the teacher; and hence those portions are given in parantheses).

chant—

अभिवादये (वैश्वामित्र, आघमर्षण, कौशिक, त्रय-) आर्षेय प्रवरान्वित, (कौशिक) गोत्रः (आपस्तंब) सूत्रः, (यजुः) शाखाध्यायी, श्री (कृष्णशर्मा) नामाहं अस्मि भोः ॥

Abhivādaye (Vaiśvāmitra, Āghamarṣaṇa, Kauśika, traya-) ārṣeya pravarānvita (Kauśika) gotraḥ, (Āpastamba) sūtraḥ, (Yajuḥ) śākhādhyāyī, śrī (kṛṣṇa śarmā) nāmāham asmi bhoḥ.

O all-formed Devi, I salute your lotus feet. I am born in the *gotraḥ* which has (*Viśvāmitra, Āghamarṣaṇa, Kauśika*) ṛṣi-triad as the patriarchs. I follow the (*Āpastamba*) sūtra and study (*Yajur*) Veda. I am called (*Śrī Kṛṣṇa Śarmā*).

19. दिग्देवता-वन्दनम् ॥ *Digdevatā-vandanam*

Prostration to the deities of the directions.

Stand facing the same direction as in No.15, Turn round and make obeisance to the deities of the four directions etc.

प्राच्यैदिशे नमः । दक्षिणायै दिशे नमः । प्रतीच्यै दिशे नमः । उदीच्यै दिशे नमः ॥ ऊर्ध्वाय नमः । अधराय नमः । अन्तरिक्षाय नमः । भूम्यै नमः । ब्रह्मणे नमः । विष्णवे नमः । मृत्यवे नमः ।

Prācyai diśe namaḥ. Dakṣiṇāyai diśe namaḥ. Pratīcyai diśe namaḥ. Udīcyai diśe namaḥ. Ūrdhvāya namaḥ Adharāya namaḥ. Antarīkṣāya namaḥ. Bhoomyai namaḥ. Bṛahmaṇe namaḥ. Viṣṇave namaḥ. Mṛtyave namaḥ.

Obeisance to the deities of east, south, west, north, above, below, middle and earth. Obeisance to *Brahmā, Viṣṇu* and *Rudraḥ*.

20. यमवन्दनम् || *Yama vandanam*

Prostration to the Lord of Death.

Stand facing south, palms joined.

यमाय नमः । यमाय धर्मराजाय मृत्यवे च अन्तकाय च । वैवस्वताय कालाय सर्वभूतक्षयाय च । औदुम्बराय दध्नाय नीलाय परमेष्ठिने । वृकोदराय चित्राय चित्रगुप्ताय वै नमः ॥ चित्रगुप्ताय वै नम ओं नम इति ॥

Yamāya namaḥ.
Yamāya dharmarājāya mṛtyave cāntakāya ca.
Vaivasvatāya kālāya sarvabhūta kṣayāya ca.
Audumbarāya dadhnāya nīlāya parameṣṭhine.
Vṛkodarāya citrāya citraguptāya vai namaḥ.
Citraguptāya vai nama om nama iti.

Obeisance to *Yamaḥ* who controls everything, who is the Lord of *dharma*, who is death and who is Time, who disintegrates all beings, who is very powerful, who is called *dadhna*, who is black in complexion, who is worshipped by all, who has an ample stomach, who keeps secrets marvellously and who is a wonder himself. Obeisance again to *Citragupta*.

21. हरिहरवन्दनम् || *Harihara vandanam*

Prostration to *Harihara*

Stand facing west.

ऋतँ सत्यं परं ब्रह्म पुरुषं कृष्णपिङ्गलम् । ऊर्ध्वरेतं विरूपाक्षं विश्वरूपाय वै नमः ।। विश्वरूपाय वै नम ओं नम इति ।।

Ṛtam satyam param brahma puruṣam kṛṣṇa piṅgalam. Ūrdhvaretam virūpākṣam viśvarūpāya vai namaḥ. Viśvarūpāya vai nama om nama iti.

I bow down before *Harihara* who is Parabrahman, the ground of beauty in all visible things, who pervades all bodies, who is the confluence of the darkness of *Viṣṇu,* and the redness of *Śiva,* who transcends sex, who is three-eyed, and all-formed. Obeisance again and again to the all-formed.

22. सूर्यनारायणवन्दनम् || *Sūryanārāyaṇa vandanam*

Prostration to *Sūryanārāyaṇa*

नमः सवित्रे जगदेकचक्षुषे जगत् प्रसूति स्थितिनाश हेतवे त्रयीमयाय त्रिगुणात्मधारिणे विरिंचि नारायण शंकरात्मने ।। ध्येयः सदा सवितृमण्डल मध्यवर्ती

नारायणः सरसिजासन संनिविष्टः ।

केयूरवान् मकरकुण्डलवान् किरीटी

हारी हिरण्मयवपुर्धृत शंख चक्रः ॥

शंख चक्र गदापाणे द्वारकानिलयाच्युत ।

गोविन्द पुण्डरीकाक्ष रक्ष मां शरणागतम् ॥

आकाशात् पतितं तोयं यथा गच्छति सागरम् ।

सर्वदेव-नमस्कारः केशवं प्रतिगच्छति ॥

केशवं प्रतिगच्छति ओं नम इति ॥

Now as in No.18, chant

अभिवादये... भोः ॥

Namaḥ savitre jagateka cakṣuṣe

jagat prasūti sthiti nāśa hetave

trayīmayāya triguṇātma dhariṇe

viriñci nārāyaṇa saṅkarātmane.

Dhyeyaḥ sadā savitṛmaṇḍala madhyavartī

nārāyaṇaḥ sarasijāsana saṁniviṣṭaḥ ।

Keyūravān makarakuṇḍalavān kirīṭī

hārī hiraṇmayavapurdhṛta śaṅkha cakraḥ ॥

Śaṅkha cakra gadāpāṇe dvārakānilayācyuta ।

Govinda puṇḍarīkākṣa rakṣa mām śaraṇāgatam ॥

Ākāśāt patitam toyam yathā gacchati sāgaram ।

sarvadeva namaskāraḥ keśavam pratigacchati ||
Keśavam pratigacchati om nama iti ||

Now as in No.18 , chant
Abhivādaye... bhoḥ ||

Salutations to the sun who functions as the sole eye of the world, who is the cause of the creation, sustentation, and dissolution of the worlds, who is of the form of the Veda, and who appears as *Brahmā, Viṣṇu* and *Śiva* by the manifestation of the three guṇas.

We must always meditate on *Nārāyaṇa,* who is centred in the solar orb, who is seated on a lotus in the *padmāsana* pose, who is decked with bracelet, earrings shaped like Makara fish, with head adorned by a crown, with a garland of flowers dangling on His breast, sporting the conch and discus and whose complexion rivals gold.

May I who have taken refuge in Thee be protected by Thee, who sports the conch, discus and mace, whose permanent abode is *Dvāraka,* who protects the whole universe and whose eyes rival the lotus.

Just as all the waters that fall from the sky inescapably reach the sea, all salutations to all the deities reach only *Keśava*; indeed they reach only *Keśava.*

O all-formed... as in No.18.chant

23. समर्पणम् | *Samarpaṇam*

Dedication

Sit down, take a little water in the palm and pour it down through the fingers after reciting the following mantra.

कायेन वाचा मनसेन्द्रियैर्वा बुद्ध्यात्मना वा प्रकृतेः स्वभावात् ।
करोमि यद्यत् सकलं परस्मै नारायणायेति समर्पयामि ॥

Kāyena vācā manasendriyair vā buddhyātmanā vā prakṛteḥ svabhāvāt ।
Karomi yadyat sakalam parasmai nārāyaṇāyeti samarpayāmi ॥

I dedicate to the Supreme person *Nārāyaṇa* all that I do by means of the body, words, mind, the organs of action, the organs of knowledge and by the impulsion of nature.

Do *ācamanam.*

24. रक्षा ॥ *Rakṣā*

Protection.

Chanting the following mantra, sprinkle a little water at the spot where the japa was performed. Then touch that spot with the ring finger and touch the forehead between the eyebrows.

अद्या नो देवसवितः प्रजावत् सावीः सौभगम् । परा दुष्वप्न्यँ सुव ॥
विश्वानि देव सवितर्दुरितानि परा सुव । यद्भद्रं तन्म आसुव ॥

Adyā no devasavitaḥ prajāvat sāvīḥ saubhagaṁ. Parā duṣvapnyam suva ||
Viśvāni devạ savitarduritāni parā suva. Yadbhadram tanma āsuva.

O *Savitā*, deign to bestow on us prosperity including many children. Please remove the cause and the effects of bad dreams. Please remove all sins; bestow on us what is good for us.